D1492072

Down Your Street

by

Jean Gumbrell

Part One

SAFFRON WALDEN

Copyright © 1989 by Jean Gumbrell

All rights reserved. No part of this publication may be reproduced, stored in a retrieval system, or transmitted in any form or by any means, electronic, mechanical, photocopying, recorded or otherwise, without the prior permission of the Copyright owner.

ISBN   0   9514542   0   X

Printed by Hart-Talbot Printers,
Saffron Walden, Essex

Foreword

Here is an opportunity for readers of Jean Gumbrell's weekly series **Down Your Street** to renew their acquaintance with some of the townspeople she has interviewed during the past five years. She visited old and new streets where a newcomer may live next door to the latest member of a family whose name has been familiar here for generations. Her warm and genuine interest in people has usually, after some initial shyness, brought a ready response with nostalgic experience of earlier days here, or perhaps fascinating glimpses of a faraway world. All neighbourliness strengthens the identity of an old community which is being tested by the doubling of its population since the 1950s, a nearby motorway, the Third London Airport, and the hi-tech industry that has opened-up rural East Anglia. However, Walden has faced other such challenges.

Forty years ago it responded generously to the needs of 2,000 London evacuees, and hundreds of American airmen will remember its friendly centre. So with a wisely controlled expansion, this great diversity of its citizens will surely enrich our lives.

For the newcomer, this book is a good introduction to Jean Gumbrell's Walden.

Mary Whiteman   1989

*The contents of this book
and most of the
accompanying photographs
were first published
in the
Saffron Walden Weekly News*

from

*April 5th 1984
to
March 3rd 1985*

Preface

Saffron Walden has a long history. First, a Saxon settlement on a site later chosen by the Normans in the 12th century to build a church and castle. Wool and weaving brought prosperity to the town in Medieval times, to be replaced by fields of saffron crocuses, changing "Chepyng Walden" to "Saffron Walden". In time malting replaced saffron, an industry which reached its peak in the 19th century and continued into the early decades of the 20th. Agriculture has always been the backdrop to life in Saffron Walden, but the demise of the old Cattle Market in 1982 meant the true meaning, of "market town", as far as Walden was concerned, was no longer applicable.

Saffron Walden has changed and even as I write this Saffron Walden is still changing. Old family businesses, which, in 1984, seemed so firmly established that one felt they would continue almost forever, have either closed down or been sold. And many of the elderly citizens interviewed for this series have alas, died. I therefore, make no apologies for the fact that many people will find this book a little out of date. After all that is what nostalgia is all about.

Jean Gumbrell

This book is dedicated to the people of Saffron Walden – past and present – because – Saffron Walden is a lovely place – and because – I believe people make places!

NEED A PLUMBER?
ROBERT TYERS LTD

63A CASTLE STREET · SAFFRON WALDEN
Telephone: 27159

Services Include:
- *Plumbing Repairs and Alterations*
- *Showers, Bathrooms* • *Water Softeners*
- *Boiler Changes* • *Central Heating*
- *All Fuels*

All work FULLY GUARANTEED for 18 months

Lime Tree Kitchens

THE ULTIMATE SERVICE

Our clients comments are the proof that we professionally design and expertly install your kitchen. Call in and see their letters and discuss with us how we can design your ultimate kitchen.

poggenpohl
THE ULTIMATE KITCHEN

Lime Tree Court, Saffron Walden (0799) 25900

Acknowledgements

The author wishes to express her gratitude to the following people, without whose help this book would not have been possible.

Gordon Richards, past Editor of the *Saffron Walden Weekly News*, who suggested the series and was a tower of strength in those early days. Colin Moule present editor of the *Weekly News*, for his moral support always. Di Pohlmann, Community Editor of the *Saffron Walden Weekly News*, for all her help and invaluable support. Dick Harding, staff photographer of the *Weekly News* for his superb photos. And all the staff of the *Weekly News* office at Saffron Walden for their unstinting co-operation.

Mary Whiteman, writer and journalist, for her generous help. Mr Ken Lovatt, for the loan of old rating lists. Mr Cliff Stacey local historian. Mr John Shaw-Ridler, Chief Librarian, Saffron Walden Library, and all his staff, especially Senior Library Assistant Martyn Everett. Mr Len Pole, Curator of Saffron Walden Museum. Sheila Jordain Assistant Curator and Maureen Evans Press Officer of Saffron Walden Museum. Mr Malcolm White, Town Clerk and his assistant Mrs Helena Whysall. Local architect Mr Donald Purkiss and local estate agent Mr Bruce Munro. And to all who have given up precious time for interviews and taken endless trouble providing information for the articles in this book.

The author also wishes to thank Essex County Library for permission to reproduce photographs in the Victorian Studies Centre at the Town Library Saffron Walden. And Cambridge

Newspapers for the majority of the photographs which appear in the book. And all who have loaned personal photographs to make the series more interesting.

She would also like to thank Cambridge Newspapers for the design of the dust cover, and Promotions Manager Gerry Spelman for his help in marketing the book. Mr Ken Wood Managing Director of Hart-Talbot Printers Ltd, whose personal involvement in the production of this book and invaluable advice on all matters has been greatly appreciated.

She would like to express her gratitude to all advertisers in the book, who have thus enabled it to be priced economically. Above all her especial thanks to her friend Kate France who so nobly volunteered to help with the advertising. And lastly to her husband Michael Gumbrell for all his encouragement and support.

Jean Gumbrell, Ashdon 1989

Sources

Department of Environment Notes on Listed Buildings (Town Library)

Mrs Dorothy Monteith's Thesis (Town Library)

Harts' Almanacks 1853/1967 (Town Library)

Journals of the Saffron Walden Antiquarian Society

Saffron Crocus – Stanley Wilson (out of print)

Saffron Walden in Old Photographs – H. C. Stacey

Saffron Walden Portrait of a Market Town – Anna Brooker & Mary Whiteman

Saffron Walden Then and Now – C. B. Rowntree (out of print)

Saffron Walden Rating Lists

The Saffron Crocus (Saffron Walden Museum Leaflet No. 13)

Saffron Walden Personalities (Saffron Walden Museum Leaflet No. 12)

Town Trail (Saffron Walden Museum Leaflet No. 1)

Saffron Walden Motors Ltd.

66 High Street, Saffron Walden, Essex CB10 1EE.
Telephone: (0799) 23597

Cambridge Centre

MEMBER
Motor Agents Association

Three generations of the Hobbs family serving the community where the customer comes first.

Rover Group

Today's cars for Today's people

METRO   MAESTRO   MINI

ROVER 800   ROVER 200

50 years
1938 – 1988

Contents

ESTABLISHED OVER 100 YEARS

GRAY PALMER LTD

High Street, Saffron Walden
Telephone: 22159

FULL HIRE SERVICE

*Formal and evening
1000 suits in stock*

- Boss
- Oder mark
- Mr Harry
- Magee

SHIRTS

- Van Heusen
- Peter England
- Raelbrook

CASUAL WEAR

- Levi
- Wrangler
- Gabicci

LADIES CASUALS

- Falmer
- Levi

FULL SHOE Dept
FULL BOYS Dept

*As big as a
department store
As friendly as a
Village Shop*

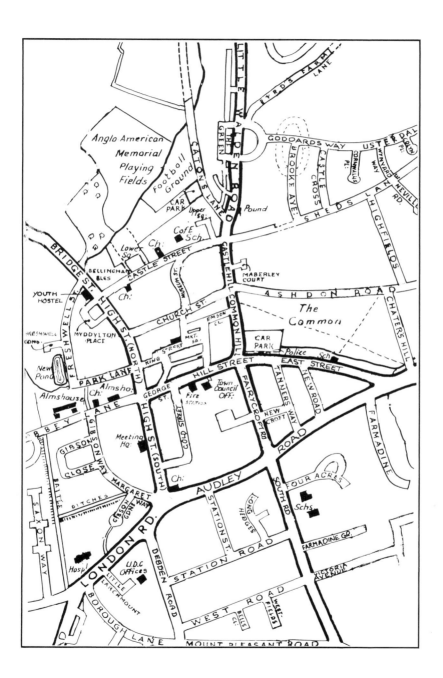

Pictures Down Your Street

The finest selection
of bone china tableware
and giftware,
full lead crystal
and
specialist cookware

EXPRESSION 1

51 HIGH STREET SAFFRON WALDEN ESSEX CB10 1AR

CHAPTER ONE

The High Street

First published in the Saffron Walden Weekly News
April 5 – May 24, 1984

Perhaps no other street in the town better reflects the changing history of Saffron Walden than its High Street.

Running from north to south of the town, its houses and buildings span more than six centuries of architecture.

Small 14th and 15th century cottages nudge elbows with elegant Georgian facades; splendid early Victorian town mansions contrast with their later Gothic counterparts; Tudor beams and 20th century brick are all to be found in the High Street.

Dating back to Saxon times; it is a street which has evolved slowly, keeping pace with the lives of the townspeople, yet never an important shopping centre in the whole of its life.

At one time it was three streets; Cuckingstool End Street at the top of the hill by the war memorial, running down to George Street; Middle Ward from George Street to King Street, and the High Street proper from the Cross Keys Hotel to the junction of Castle Street.

It is at this junction where we will start our walk, at No. 1, a building which was once Thomas Barcham's Grocer's shop from 1873 until 1914.

Across the road stands The Close, a splendid timber-framed house dating back to the 15th century with a curious "spider window", like an all-seeing eye looking out on to the changing world.

A second wing was added to The Close at some time during the 16th century, which was to be entirely encased in brick in 1854 by Francis Gibson, who was at that time living there.

This wing was completely dismantled in 1934 and subsequently removed and re-erected in West Grinstead, Sussex, where it is now known as "Walden Close."

Francis Gibson was the youngest son of the Quaker, Atkinson Francis Gibson, a land surveyor who married the daughter of Jabez Wyatt, a wealthy brewer who lived at No.7 High Street.

Francis Atkinson Gibson had three sons, Wyatt George, Jabez and Francis. Francis was the artistic member of the Gibson family and a keen landscape gardener. He married Elizabeth Pease in 1829 and went to live at The Close in 1854.

The high-walled garden at The Close proved too restricting for his hobby so he purchased land behind Castle Street where he designed the gardens now known as Bridge End Gardens.

His intention was to have an underground passage leading from The Close to the gardens but for some unknown reason the idea never materialised.

A manorial survey of Walden dated 1600 shows the house clearly marked as "Priors"; this would appear to be the earliest recorded name for this property as it was originally intended to house the priests serving the Parish Church, and at one time part of the building was actually used as a chapel.

At one period in its history it was known as "Baron House", presumably because it was reputed to have been built by an ancestor of the Baron family, an old-established local family whose monument in the Parish Church indicates that they were living in Walden during the 17th century.

According to the present owner of The Close, Mrs. Anne Fotherby, Thomas More's widow is supposed to have lived in the house at some time, and 'another fairy story,' she adds with a laugh, 'Judge Jeffreys' widow is also supposed to have lived here.'

The spider window, perhaps one of the most intriguing features of The Close, was added probably during the reign of Queen Anne, 'as a fashionable whim of those times,' says Mrs. Fotherby.

From about the turn of this present century to the outbreak of the First World War, the Sisters of Jesus and Mary ran a Convent School on the premises.

2

It was here that a certain Miss Cecily Ann Pallett from Ashdon, later to become Mrs. Frank Fordham of Bendysh Hall, Radwinter, first received her grounding in music, which was to form the second love of her life, her first love being the life of a farmer's wife.

In 1914 the Convent was closed down and the Sisters of Jesus and Mary went to help nurse the wounded at Walden Place. Later, the barn belonging to The Close was converted into the present-day Catholic Church in Castle Street, and the coach house became the Pentecostal Hall.

Anne Fotherby came to The Close as a young wife in 1955. She and her husband had arrived in Saffron Walden six years earlier when her husband took up his appointment as Treasurer to what was then the Rural District Council.

When the southern wing of the Close was pulled down in 1934, money was raised by public subscription to buy the site and in 1936, a tiny walled garden was opened to the public.

This delightful little park offers blissful respite to the foot-weary. And even on a bleak day in late winter, it provides a small sheltered oasis bursting with the promise of spring and the noise of the birds.

Opposite the garden stands No.5 High Street, an imposing brick-faced house of economically elegant proportions dating back to the reign of Queen Anne, re-faced and extended during the 19th century.

Many people will remember this house as the home and surgery of the late Dr. S.R. Richardson during the 30s and 40s.

Part of the garden of No.5 has been given over to the erection of a neo-Georgian residence built as a sympathetic addition to the existing properties.

Adjoining this, a modern town house, created from part of the wing of No.7, again adding 20th century character to the surrounding architecture.

No.7 is a late 18th century town mansion; its original red brick covered with grey stucco in the late 19th century.

This was the home of the brewer, Jabez Wyatt, whose daughter, Elizabeth, married Francis Atkinson Gibson, son of George Gibson, a successful mid-18th century draper and upholsterer, who owned considerable amounts of property and land in and around Saffron Walden.

After his marriage to Jabez Wyatt's daughter, Atkinson Francis took over his father-in-law's brewery next door and became a prosperous brewer and maltster. His three sons all became prominent men, playing vital roles in the life of the town.

Adjoining No.7 and the brewery, and believed to have been the brewery manager's house at one time, are two narrow house fronts, each with 16th century carved panels on the doors.

At No.7A lives Mr. Peter Paget and his family, the town's very first SDP Alliance Councillor. Recently Mr. Paget stripped the paint from the kitchen door of No.7A and discovered the initial JG carved at the height of a child on the honey-coloured woodwork.

'Possibly,' he says, 'these were the young Jabez Gibson's initials when he lived here.'

From the attics of the brewery manager's house the sad crumbling sight of the old brewery roofs can be seen.

Tragically neglected for want of a little attention, this historic timberwork is being left to rot.

Lending an air of almost bucolic charm to the Hight Street Nos.4 and 6 are an interesting example of an early 14th century Essex Hall House.

For many years two separate dwellings they were once the home of Wyatt George Gibson, who probably moved there after his marriage to Deborah Stacey in 1817. It was here at No.6 that his son George Stacey Gibson was born, the best remembered and respected member of the Gibson family.

Wyatt George was very much involved with local government and it was he who provided the town with the hospital in London Road.

He left No.6 in 1827 to move further along the High Street, and it must have been shortly after this that John Burton, a saddler arrived to carry out his business at these premises.

According to the town Almanack for 1853, John Burton had already been established for 71 years by then, and succeeding generations of Burtons were to continue in his footsteps until the latter part of the 1930s.

At an auction sale on April 20th, 1920 at 4.15pm precisely, in Saffron Walden Town Hall, a firm of local motor engineers

Herbert Burton saddler (1863-1937) outside his shop at 6 High Street, son of George Burton and grandson of John Burton

bought "a commercial property known as – The Brewery – frontage of 143 feet on to the High Street with dwelling house and offices, together with stabling for 14 horses."

It was a sign of the times, the end of one era and the beginning of another. Horses never did fill those stables again, the motor car had arrived for good.

The brewery which had once belonged to Jabez Wyatt, now belonged to young Bill Raynham and his partners.

Bill Raynham whose real name was Archibald Nelson Raynham, was a Suffolk farmer's son who went out to South Africa before the First World War to seek his fortune in farming, but returned to this country at the commencement of hostilities and enlisted in the Royal Gloucester Hussars Yeomanry.

In 1917 he was wounded and invalided out of the army to spend the remainder of the war with the Ministry of Agriculture. His job chiefly concerned with farm machinery convinced him that there was a future in the mechanical side of farming.

So, after the war he formed a partnership with two other

Joseph Wright's Shop, later known as North Essex Motor Company, now the site of Woolworths

farmers, and bought The North Essex Motor Company, a business which stood on the site now occupied by Woolworths.

Originally intending to sell Fordson tractors, future trends could be seen, and they quickly turned over to the sale of cars. In those early days, Raynhams held the agencies for all the most popular makes of car, names that are now just a nostalgic memory for the older generation – Coventry Eagle, Humber, Wolf, Singer and Standard.

After nearly 40 successful years in the trade Bill Raynham began to prepare for retirement and make way for his son John to step into his shoes, although it was to be some time before John was to take over the reins entirely. Mr. C.C.Hirst, who had been with the company since 1937, had been joint Managing Director for a number of years, and was to continue as Managing Director until his death in 1980.

Mr. Hirst will be remembered by many people in Saffron Walden, as will Mr. Arthur Thake also, who died a few years ago.

It was Arthur Thake who, before the Second World War, drove Raynhams' coaches and had the responsibility of taking the local football team to their venue, 'and what was more important', says John Raynham, 'getting them back home again!'

Mr. Raynham continues, 'actually we are very fortunate in that a lot of our employees are very loyal and stop with us for years. Men like our workshop foreman Mr. Newbold and stores department manager Eric Rust who have worked for the company nearly all their working lives. Whilst our Mr. James Roberts, who has been friend and mentor to countless learner-drivers in and around the town, has also been with us for well over 20 years.'

'And it would be impossible to talk about the company without mentioning Mrs. D.M. Wakeford who first came to work in the office 50 years ago and eventually became Company Secretary, and although now retired, is still Company Secretary.'

'It is also interesting to note,' says Mr. Raynham, 'that Mr. Phillip Gowlett, one of our directors, is the son of one of the

Raynhams 1920s.

7

original farmers who co-founded the firm, and another director, Mr. Peter Cowell, the grandson of the other founder.'

And now, to add to the continuity of this long-established business which has become a household name in a town almost unique for its number of old-established family businesses, James Raynham, John's 21 year-old son has recently joined the company, representing the third generation of Raynhams.

A comparative newcomer to the High Street however, is the Saffron Hotel, although its origins date back in parts to the 16th century.

Once three separate houses, Nos.8, 10 and 12, many times altered and refaced, were eventually turned into one hotel in the 1950s called "The Old House" and later "The Saffron Hotel".

During the early part of this century Robert Oxborrow boot and shoe-maker lived at No.12, to be succeeded by his daughters, the Misses Oxborrow, dressmakers noted for their meticulous workmanship and serviceable clothes.

The Misses Oxborrow were still there in 1941, no doubt making-do-and-mending for the clothes conscious ladies of Saffron Walden in wartime.

But for the past four years the Saffron Hotel has been run by the Craddock family. The proprietor, Mr. Ronald Craddock, a young man in his 30s trained as a chef at The Grosvenor Hotel in London, and at the age of 19 was the youngest chef with the highest qualifications at that time.

A delightful feature of the restaurant of The Saffron Hotel is a tiny paved courtyard entered by means of french windows off the dining room. The surrounding timber-framed and weather-boarded buildings overlooking this courtyard are believed to have belonged to a former maltings, which could account for the high carriage-way arch on the south side of No.10.

Victoria House, situated on the corner of High Street and Church Street is an elegant 19th century house of pleasing proportions proving that the Victorians were not always tasteless philistines.

On the opposite corner stands Cambridge House, the site

of what was once one of the most important hostelries in the town – The White Hart. It was here the Samuel Pepys stayed in 1660 when he paid his historic visit to Audley End House.

Sadly, this old inn was pulled down in the 19th century but it is believed that much of the original interior still remains. Now the Magistrates Court and Register Office, it will be remembered by many as a welfare centre for evacuees and the British Restaurant during the Second World War.

(British Restaurants were set up to supplement the meagre food rations of those years. Simple, well-cooked meals could be obtained at reasonable prices and either eaten on the premises or, alternatively, providing you brought along your own dishes, purchased and taken away.)

Go back 60 years and we find that Cambridge House was "an old-established private boarding and day school for girls, conducted upon the best high principles" by the Misses Gowlett.

How many of those high-principled young ladies remain in Walden today? Three at the very least!

Miss Kathleen and Miss Gladys Trigg, both now in their 90s remember Cambridge House School during the first decade of this century. Their sister, Mollie remembers it in the early 20s. 'Not,' she says with a laugh, 'the happiest time of my life. It was alright if you were a favourite but I never was!'

But the Miss Triggs can trace the history of Cambridge House School further back than that. There is a faded photograph in their possession which shows their mother as a pupil of Cambridge House in 1887, when the headmistress was a Mrs. Barrett, and it was known as "an academy for young ladies."

For a short while Kathleen and Gladys were boarders at the school, and their reminiscences are a fascinating vignette of life at a girls school before the First World War.

'In 1906 the headmistress was Miss Rose Cowell,' says Kathleen Trigg, 'and her sister Laurie, the housekeeper, also taught the juniors. They took small boys as well as older girls.

'When we were there in 1906-8, girls were coached for Cambridge Local Exams, but had to sit for them at the Friends' School.

'The local church organist, Dr. Mahon, came to give music

lessons to a few. For tennis we went to a court in Radwinter Road under the shadow of the gasometer, and we were allowed to use the Grammar School Gymnasium.'

The Miss Cowells instilled into their pupils very high principles indeed, and one lesson Kathleen and Gladys Trigg learned has remained in their minds ever since: "A little thing is a little thing, but faithfulness in a little thing is a big thing."

'But everything was rather different when I went back to teach in 1916' continues Kathleen Trigg, 'by then the three Miss Gowletts had taken over, and the building had been altered considerably. The youngest Miss Gowlett had been a pupil-teacher in my mother's day.'

'It was a very cold place during those war years, often we had to wash in cold water, and although the maids were allowed hot water bottles, the teachers were not. We were not even allowed to make ourselves hot drinks before going to bed at night.

'We overcame this problem by secretly brewing ourselves hot drinks on a tiny stove in the teachers common room. The Miss Gowletts' would have had a fit if they'd found out.'

But towards the latter-part of the 1920's the Miss Gowletts moved their high-principled young ladies to a house called "The Grove" (now Eastacre) over-looking the Common.

Next door to Cambridge House stands a small timber-framed gem. Nos. 18 and 20 are believed to have been a weaver's cottage dating back to the early 16th century (suggested by the small leaded windows high under the eaves).

At one time steps led up to the front door but these were removed when the cellar was filled in and floor lowered to give more ceiling height.

Known as "The Army and Navy Stores", the present proprietor Mr.Peter Evans has gradually managed to eliminate the "army surplus" image during the 11 years he has been in business on the premises. He now specialises in reasonably priced but high quality casual clothes and camping equipment, for which he says there is an increasing demand.

No country market town is complete without its gun shop, and at No. 17 Russell Walkyier carries on the business his father started in 1965.

From the outside it is a tiny, unassuming little shop; inside all is activity – not to be confused with urgency. For, a man buying a gun must not be hurried.

He must have time to hold it in his hands; feel the weight; squint down the barrel; test the action and linger over and appreciate the quality of the craftmanship.

With the warm glow of pine-clad walls and dark, serviceable carpet on the floor it could be the gun room of a country house; even to the yellow labrador snoring noisily on the floor before the fire.

Russell Walkyier and his dogs

Everywhere there is the exciting clutter which goes with guns and "gunny" people, as Russell Walkyier likes to call his customers. Notwithstanding the clutter, everything is pin-clean and spotless, the guns displayed gleaming with the loving care lavished upon them.

Russell Walkyier does not apologise for the clutter. 'Gunny people like to feel at home when they come in here. They like to come in with their muddy boots and know it doesn't matter,' he says. 'They want to browse around and perhaps sit down for a while and have a bit of a yarn.'

No. 17, like most of the property nearby, dates back to before the 17th century; difficult to say how far back, but from the Manorial Survey of 1600, it appears to have been part of, if not wholly, a bakehouse.

Later it became an addition to the Old Brewery, and latterly the local branch of the Westminister Bank.

Think of bakehouses and one automatically thinks of Coles and Christmas puddings.

Seven years ago Albert John Cole found an old family recipe for a Christmas Pudding going back over 150 years, and being the extraordinary far-sighted entrepreneur he is, he was quick to realise its potential.

That is how Coles Traditional Christmas Puddings were born, an amazing family enterprise which now enjoys a high-standing reputation both at home and abroad.

Since Coles started producing their Traditional Christmas puddings, their turnover has increased manyfold and letters of appreciation come flooding in from all over the world.

But the story of A.J. Cole and Sons goes back further than that, and is a fascinating story of courage, hardwork and enterprise.

Albert John Cole was a Colchester man who, during the grim days of depression after the First World War took the only job he could get – in a bakery. He worked hard, long hours for a meagre pittance, but those grey years of graft and grind were to stand him in good stead, and he soon became a highly skilled master-baker.

In a bid to improve himself he moved to Great Chesterford and worked for Mr. Searle the local baker whose turnover he quickly increased.

But Albert's wife felt her husband deserved better and encouraged him to look around for his own business. Hearing this, Mr. Searle begged Albert to stay on. Instead, Albert offered to buy the business.

The offer was accepted, and somehow or other the Coles managed to raise the capital, no easy task in the struggling days of the 30s.

From then on Albert began to reap the rewards of his early privations. Hardworking, competent and intelligent, he was able to buy other businesses in the area, and eventually bought Nos.52 and 54 High Street, Saffron Walden, which he kept supplied from his bakery in Great Chesterford.

A.W. Andrews had been the established bakers and confectioners at No. 91 High Street for many years, but with the coming of A.J. Cole, Mr. Andrews began to feel the pinch. Realising it was useless to compete, he offered his business to Albert. That was in 1939.

Now, although still taking an active interest in the Company through his role as consultant to Coles Traditional Christmas Puddings, Albert Cole leaves the actual baking to his sons, Christopher, 37, and Timothy, 35, and their foreman Alan Doherty, all of whom are very much involved with the actual production of everything which bears the name A.J. Cole & Sons.

It is interesting to note that since the turn of the century No. 19 has always been a bakehouse and even on the manorial survey of 1600 it appears clearly marked as "The Bakehouse".

Nicholas Tsentides, a Greek Cypriot by birth, opened his Taverna at No. 21 High Street four years ago.

Previously, Nicholas and his wife sold fabrics and dress materials from these premises, but a restaurateur by profession and pioneer of Greek Tavernas outside London, Nicholas decided to return to the way of life he knew best.

For 12 years the Tsentides have been lovingly and painstakingly restoring this historic old building – believed by some to be as old as Saffron Walden itself – without any financial help from the local authorities.

Curious brick archways in the cellar lend speculation as to whether it was part of the old bakehouse or perhaps the foundations of something much older; a theory endorsed by

13

the 12th century beam across the bar in the cellar, indentical to one found in a Chelmsford Church.

And when stripping the plaster from the walls of his room, tiny, obviously original widows, indentical to the ones at No. 18/20 opposite were revealed.

Next door to the Army and Navy Stores is all that remains of a family business associated with this part of the High Street for almost 100 years.

Gone are the days when Barnard Brothers, Corn and Coal Merchants brewed their own beer for the men who drove their heavy horse-drawn drays beneath the archway which now leads to nowhere.

Still in existence however, but no longer in the High Street, Barnard Brothers are now run by the fourth and fifth generation of that family.

George Herbert Barnard was a prosperous farmer of Newport and it was his sons, Sidney, Herbert and Ernest who founded the firm in 1854.

Originally corn merchants, their coal dealing evolved from a natural sequence of providing a service for small local farmers, and they soon became a household name in Saffron Walden until that part of the business was discontinued at sometime during the 1970s, when the old maltings were demolished and replaced by smart town houses.

Radio Supply Stores at No. 25 is again a family business. Once Joseph's Wright's cycle shop before he moved across the road to where Woolworths now stands, it was bought in 1915 by William Wells a Barking man, who also sold bicycles and radio spares (from whence the shop gets its name).

When William Wells fell ill, in 1918, his son Horace came to live above the shop with his wife, and carried on the business until his own death in 1934, when once again the business was sold.

In 1950 a young man called John Jacobs entered the firm as a junior service engineer and later bought the company which he now runs in conjunction with his wife Parma and brother Gordon.

Again the actual fabric of the building can be traced back over the centuries. And it was here in 1900 that yet another family business started, when Walter Charles Bunting set up

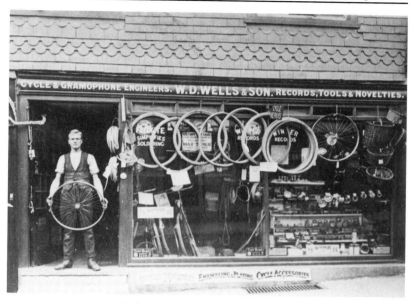

Radio Supply Stores as it was in 1918.

his greengrocery enterprise, which he later moved to Stansted where it is now carried on by his grandsons. From the turn of the century until 1969 Nos. 27 and 29 High Street were the site of Cro's Market Stores.

Started in 1900 by Benjamin Cro himself and spanning the swiftly moving decades of the 20th century, Cro's Stores will be remembered and mourned by many of the older generation in Saffron Walden.

"The Cheapest and most Reliable Establishment in the District" proclaimed their advertisement in 1910. Cro's Stores must have been one of Saffron Walden's greatest assets for, not only did they sell grocery, provisions, biscuits and cakes, patent medicines, cigars and tobacco, furniture of all description, plus all kinds of carpets, linoleum and floor coverings, but they also undertook French polishing and "repairs of all kinds" on the premises! A mind-boggling undertaking for what must have been a comparatively small building.

But the motor-car obviously sounded the ultimate death knell for Cro's, although it was to survive for a few more years in new premises in Church Street. Nevertheless during its lifetime it carved an irreplaceable niche in the memory of many local people, never to be fully replaced by any modern counterparts.

No.30 High Street is the Electricity Showrooms known as "The County of London Electric Supply Company" during the 30s and 40s.

Joined to the Cross Keys Hotel next door by enormous beams, the building obviously suffered damage at the time the roof to the Cross Keys was raised during the 18th century.

Tiny doorways, sloping floors and cock-eyed window all seem to bear evidence of this.

According to the museum leaflet "Town Trail" the Cross Keys Hotel was originally two houses, probably dating back to the 14th century in parts. Popular opinion generally accepts that it is a 16th century Inn and historical records date back to about that period.

At one time the whole of this picturesque timber-framed building was covered in plaster, and purists insist that this is the authentic treatment for East Anglian houses of this type.

However, it is also accepted that before the 16th century, substantially built timber-framed buildings were not plastered. Plastering, to provide extra warmth and protection, became a fashionable feature of that century.

The Cross Keys, rightly or wrongly, was stripped of its plaster around 1910 and remains today, one of the most attractive buildings in the High Street.

According to local historian Mr. Clifford Stacey, in 1709 the Cross Keys was known as the Bulls Head, and at one time was described as a "Baking Office."

During the time of the Civil War, Royalist prisoners were brought to the Cross Keys when first captured and locked up in one of the upstairs rooms before being despatched on their way. And it is said that the Inn is haunted by one of Cromwell's guards whose ghostly footsteps can be heard patrolling the passage-ways in the dead of night.

A worthy ghost, who has earned the Cross Keys honourable mention in the American publication "The Good Ghost Guide".

The proprietor, Mr. Tony Knott, says it is incredible how

16

many people come to stay at the hotel purely because they have been told it is haunted.

Whilst standing on the east side of the street, it is worth pausing for a few moments to look at the shops across the road, all of them historically and architecturally interesting.

The original High Street ends, incongruously, with one of the most strident examples of 20th century architecture.

How many people remember, I wonder, the fine old Georgian house, home of the Miss Claydens which was pulled down in 1934 to make way for what is now the Co-op Supermarket?

The Miss Claydens were ladies of "the old school" who filled the splendid Regency windows of their home with bowls of beautiful flowers and were deeply involved with the life of the town.

'I can always remember,' says Miss Kathleen Trigg, 'seeing Hilda Clayden at the age of 70 playing tennis in white boots!'

The Miss Claydens did not disappear with their house however, but moved higher up the street to continue their life of gracious living in a fast-changing world for a few more years.

———— · ————

In 1758 it was called Middle Ward, but we know it today as that part of the High Street between King Street and George Street on the east side, and Park Lane and Abbey Lane on the west side.

To get from Middle Ward to Cuckingstool End Street (now High Street south) one would have had to cross King's Ditch (the Slade) by means of footbridges one on either side of the street.

Called King's Bridge, these are clearly marked on the 1750 map of Saffron Walden. Later, when the Slade was covered over, the name was transferred to an adjacent street (probably called Market End Street in the 17th century) and King Street came into being.

At the beginning of the 17th century, the Swanne Inne, another of the town's important hostelries, stood where the Post Office now stands.

Department of Environment records describe the present building as "an early 17th century house, many times altered during the 18th and 19th centuries."

It was once the home of Dr. J.P. Atkinson Senior, a distinguished local doctor who bought the property in 1881 and lived there until his death in 1917.

Now standing squarely between two extremes of modern 20th century architecture the Post Office displays a brave face to the rest of the High Street.

Sadly, this is all that is left of a once splendid old building – just a distinguished Georgian facade; even the wrought iron balcony which once graced the canopy over the main entrance has been removed.

The present Post Office was opened on this site in 1919 after its removal from King Street (now W.H. Smith's) and during the early 70s the whole of the inside of the building was completely gutted, leaving just the facade intact.

At the same time, a historically interesting old staircase was removed to be subsequently installed in the old primary school at Langley Upper Green.

Since then the old school has changed hands. However, Mr. Stanley Jennings, the previous owner, assures me that the staircase was not the original staircase belonging to the Swanne Inne, but a pine staircase, dated, according to the British Museum, at about 1720, and believed to have come from Audley End House probably at the time the mansion was altered in the late 18th century, when an existing staircase was removed and replaced by one of stone.

Both staircases are identical says Mr. Jennings, and this would appear to support his theory.

Whilst the Post Office site was beign excavated, an old coin was found. Now the "James I" shilling stands in a glass case on the left hand side of the Concourse.

Ernest Street's Draper's Shop is yet another well remembered family business, now gone, which stood next door to the Post Office on the side where the Co-operative Department Store now stands.

At sometime between 1896 and 1914, the Misses Hart had No. 41 High Street as a "Berlin Wool and Fancy Work Repository". Enterprising ladies the Misses Hart.

Not only did they dressmake and embroider handkerchiefs to order, but they also had a Registery Office for Servants. A sign of the times maybe, but how clever to cash in on an opportunity arising out of the very nature of their work which brought them into contact with ladies of all classes.

Later the Misses Hart moved, and probably it was then that Ernest Street took over No. 41 for his private residence.

When Mr. Wanderless took over Ernest Street's business No.41 became part of the shop and later still, in the early 1960s, another piece of Walden history disappeared in flames.

Across the road is a ladies dress shop now called Patricia's, known for many years as "Frances", but remembered by the older generation as "World Stores" in the 30s and 40s of this decade, and earlier still Walkers Stores grocers and provision merchants.

It was Walkers presumably who altered this late 18th century building with its lovely old red-tiled roof, and added the extraordinary Edwardian Gothic gable facing the High Street.

But the upper storey windows are a delight, with a curious 19th century charm.

Later, in 1954, Rumsey's opened their Bedding Centre on these premises.

Sharing this same building is Fells, a modern chemist's shop with an old-fashioned approach.

Mr. Christopher Fell was born near Liverpool and represents the fourth generation in a family of pharmacists. He says his job is not just a matter of dispensing medicines, it is far more interesting than that.

He believes that people are turning to pharmacists more and more these days because doctors are so busy and have little time to talk to their patients.

He continues, 'Often it is not a question of being ill at all, but just something on their minds, and talking things over with someone who is not personally involved is a great help to some people."

But there are those who expect their shopkeepers to be personally involved. Although Gray Palmer, at No. 47 High Street is as modern as tomorrow, and many times larger than its external appearance would have us believe, it still retains an old-fashioned personal touch built up throughout the years by a loyal staff who make it their business to get to know and understand their customer's tastes and needs.

Men like Mr. Harry Cox, who will be remembered by many of Gray Palmer's older customers, and who spanned three generations of the Palmer family, finally retiring after 67 years service. And Mr. Bert Sillett, who will also be well-remembered by many people in the Saffron Walden area, and who worked for this family business for forty-seven years.

Gray Palmer's in its early days.

20

The present Manager, Mr. Fred Dare, is a comparative newcomer with only 25 years service, and Mr. Dennis Clarke, can only muster a mere 20 years!

'It is the personal touch which these assistants, their colleagues and their predecessors, convey to the many long-standing customers of Gray Palmer which is the mainstay of the business,' says Mr. Richard Gray Palmer.

'Many of our customers,' he continues, 'are ladies from the country whose husbands are unable to accompany them on shopping trips. But it is no exaggeration to say that our staff know exactly what these ladies' husbands want and their sizes too!'

Gray Palmer, grandfather of Mr. Richard, first opened his Men's Outfitters in Debden Road in 1887, moving to 47 High Street, just before the turn of the century.

It was here, above the shop, that he and his wife lived with their 11 children, the eldest of whom, William Gray Palmer was to carry on the business and in turn pass it on to his son, Richard.

In those days Gray Palmer specialised in clothes and boots for the working man, and to help pay for those clothes, he started the clothing club which his grandson still operates today.

Things have changed however since the days when nearly every farmworker wore cord trousers or a suit of Derby Tweed. Now its jeans, green wellingtons, T-shirts and all things casual.

Mr. Richard Gray Palmer entered the family business in 1949, after two years' service in the forces. Although he had previously trained to be a school teacher, he says he has never regretted entering the family firm.

'I feel I am very lucky,' he says, 'I thoroughly enjoy my work, and so few people can say that today.

'Of course there have been a lot of changes, just as there were in my father's time when he first entered the business in 1914.

'We now carry a lot more stock. During my father's time we used to keep about sixty gentlemen's suits, and these would be folded and kept on shelves. Now we stock about twelve hundred and every one of them has to have its own hanger.

21

'We also sold more hats. Everyone wore a hat in those days. We still keep hats of course, but mostly they are the country tweed type. Bowlers and trilbys are right out!'

Next door to Gray Palmer at No.49, was a shop remembered by many people in the town, especially those who, as young boys, stood, nose pressed to the window, looking at the highly professional "meccano" models which took pride of place amongst the toys and bikes on display. "Walbros Cycle Shop" started in 1910 by Victor and Percy Wallis, continued for 60 years at these premises until it sadly closed sometime about 1970.

Painted a deep and unblushing pink, Central Hall across the road from Gray Palmer, can hardly be described as one of the most attractive buildings in the High Street.

Believed to have been a small maltings at one time, it has nevertheless, played its own unique role in shaping the lives of many of the inhabitants of the town.

Certainly it shaped the destiny of one young man, Arthur Gillett, whose parents ran a greengrocery business in Cross Street.

Invited to a Girls' Club sixpenny hop at Central Hall by a young lady (the boys went free of charge) young Arthur fell under the spell of another charmer, Emma Bouch, and walked her home instead of his original sweetheart.

They were married in 1926, and after over 50 years of marriage, it would appear that Arthur did very well to walk Emma home from the sixpenny hop at Central Hall.

Earlier, in 1910, Mr. Andrew Dix opened Walden's very first cinema at these premises, to be superseded two years later by a smart, building at the top of the High Street.

The latest newcomer to the High Street is Walden Models. Twenty-six year-old Mr. Keith Marshall is an enthusiastic member of the Saffron Walden Model Railway Club.

The older generation will remember these premises as Mr. Willett's butcher's shop. Traces of these days may still be seen in the iron rail spanning the top of the window, where carcases were hung, and the marble slab bearing the date 1862 when, presumably Mr. Willett opened-up his business.

Crossing the road again we come to two of the most elegant shops in the High Street – Panache and Expression I.

22

Corner of Abbey Lane

Both shops form the ground floor of what was once The Abbey Temperance Hotel. In 1910 this hotel belonged to a Mr. Edwards who also had a coal business and "dabbled" in architecture, leaving his wife to cope with the Hotel.

It is difficult to find out much about the Abbey Hotel. D. of E. records say it is an 18th century brick-fronted building (now painted) altered during the 19th and 20th centuries. The old rating lists show that it was a private house in 1757 and between 1807 and 1824 belonged to the Searle family.

It eventually became the property of The Coffee Tavern Company in 1881 and in 1889 called The Abbey Tavern, then later The Abbey Hotel.

In the Saffron Walden Almanack for 1900 it advertises "Hot dinners delivered daily in the town at restaurant prices. Choice cooked ham always cut, 1/6d per lb (15p). Horse, trap and wagonette to let or hire."

But the image of the building has certainly changed since then. For almost four years Mrs. Myrtle Williams has been the proprietor of Panache. Why Panache?

'It is a word I use when describing people," she says.

Mrs. Williams had never worked in the dress trade before opening her shop. 'But I love clothes,' she says, 'and it gives me a thrill to see a woman walk out of the shop with something that makes her look really special and which I know she is happy with."

Next door Expression I is a shop filled with exciting and beautiful things for home-loving people. Owned and run for the past four years by ex-merchant banker Peter Walters and his wife Diana. The shop is given over entirely to china and cookware. The cookware side of the business is an extension of their hobby, both are extremely good cooks, so what could be more natural than to sell the stuff you enjoy using?

Now walking up the High Street away from the centre of the old town, the houses take on an urbane elegance, a reflection of the changing prosperity of Saffron Walden in the early 19th century.

There is still the occasional cottage to provide interesting contrast, however.

In the old days, Cuckingstool End Street was a continuation of the original High Street and Middle Ward. Or rather, it started at the Cucking Pond (Ducking Pond) approximately where Margaret Way joins the High Street on the west side, and continued to the ford at the foot of the hill.

Here it crossed the Slade (King's Ditch) and joined Middle Ward (between Abbey Lane and Park Lane). But in 1814 the name of the street was changed and it became High Street South as we know it today.

When the only means of communication with the outside world was either by foot or horse the coaches travelling daily between London and Cambridge would pass through Newport, and approach Walden from Cuckingstool End.

Almost certainly these coaches would pause at either the Greyhound or the Crowne, the two Inns which stood facing each other just before the ford.

The Crowne has long since disappeared. But the Greyhound still remains, a picturesque early 17th century building, a monument to a more leisurely age than ours, but no longer an Inn.

Old photographs show little outward change in the appearance of the building. Except, the stables, which extended down George Street as far as the smithy belonging to The George, were sacrificed some time during the 1960s to make way for a parade of shops.

The Greyhound and the Pledger family who ran it from 1880 until 1948 are remembered with affection by many Walden people.

No.48 next door to the Greyhound is one of those curiously incongruous buildings belonging neither to past nor present.

Built in 1905 by the Co-operative Wholesale Society, with little architectural empathy for its surroundings, it has been known for many years as "The Gift Shop", a wonderland of toys to delight the heart of any child.

But when the Co-operative Wholesale Society opened up their impressive new shop in 1905, selling grocery, provisions, hardware, drapery, outfitting, boots and shoes, and celebrating the event with a slap-up tea and public meeting in the Town Hall, they swept away once and for all the traces of one woman's life.

Elizabeth Butcher and her widowed mother came to live at No.48 High Street in 1877; a house belonging to George Stacey Gibson.

A glance at the old rating lists suggests that the premises would probably have been part of the Greyhound Inn complex at one time.

Described as "barn, stable and yard" in 1860; later as "house and garden" and in 1879, presumably after the death of Mrs. Butcher, "house, garden and school". From this it would be reasonable to assume that the barn was converted into a schoolhouse.

What Elizabeth Butcher's circumstances were exactly is a matter for speculation. But in an age when a woman's income could be dramatically reduced overnight, it might be supposed that James Butcher (presumably Elizabeth's brother) who shared the house with her for a short while, inherited all his father's wealth.

And rather than be an encumberance to her brother, Elizabeth did the only possible thing that a genteel lady could do – open a school for "young ladies and gentlemen".

For the next 10 years Elizabeth ran her school, buying the premises from George Stacey Gibson in 1883. However, records show that in 1890 and 1891 the house and school were empty and Elizabeth was living at her brother's house, No.60 High Street.

Had Elizabeth fallen ill? Why was she not teaching? She still owned the property. And why did Catherine and Margaret Sinclair rent it in 1896 and call it Stanmore House School?

A year later the school was being run by Elizabeth and Alice Cross, yet still owned by Elizabeth Butcher.

After 1902 there is no further record of Elizabeth Butcher. Perhaps she died or moved to another part of the town, or maybe she joined her brother.

Was James Butcher, the Walden man, who, according to the Almanack for 1896, gave a birthday party for his friends "at his residence in Chelsea", in honour of his 60th birthday, the brother of Elizabeth?

No.53 High Street is a fine early 19th century house, once the home of Dr. Hedley Bartlett.

Hedley Coward Bartlett, son of a dentist, born in London in 1863, came to Saffron Walden at the age of 18 in 1881. He was apprenticed to Dr. Henry Stear, with whom he lodged in a house in the Market Square.

In his memoirs Dr. Bartlett says that the good Dr. Stear was 'a man of few words, who taught me little, but I learned by doing things.'

After a year in the town, Hedley Bartlett returned to London to work and study at the Middlesex Hospital.

Qualifying in 1888, he came back to Saffron Walden to start his own practice and in due time became the Parish Doctor.

He was the first surgeon in Saffron Walden, and because there was no surgery in the town at that time, he performed operations on kitchen tables. Eventually, after a long struggle with the Authorities, he succeeded in getting an Operating Theatre installed in the General Hospital.

It is reputed he acquired great skill at removing cataracts from elderly eyes using the knowledge obtained from the eyes of animals supplied by local butchers, which he used for research purposes.

26

A deeply religious man, he longed to be ordained, but was refused because he was a practising doctor.

However, he did become an ordained priest in the Eastern Church in Communion with the Church of England, and opened his own "Chapel of St. Luke" at his home, where once a month his friends were invited for Holy Communion.

Dr. Hedley Bartlett retired from practice in 1936 to be succeeded by his son Dr. Justinian Bartlett, now also retired.

But we can trace the history of No.53 much further back than the esteemed Dr. Hedley Bartlett. In 1827 Wyatt George Gibson bought the house from James Searle.

James Searle was a member of the Searle family, the first bankers in Saffron Walden in the early 19th century.

Unfortunately the Searles decided to compete with the Gibson family by becoming maltsters, so the Gibsons retaliated by founding the "Saffron Walden and North Essex Bank" in 1824, resulting in the collapse of Messrs. Searle and Co., in 1825.

But even earlier than this, we discover that John Fiske another surgeon, owned a house and land on this site in 1794.

But could this possibly have been part of the old Crowne Inn? Beneath the archway joining No.53 to No.55 two-inch Tudor bricks are used as a pathway, and gargoyles set in the wall would appear to indicate a much older building than the present one.

Next door the Comrades Club at No.55 is again a splendid example of mid-19th century architecture. Little of the original house now remains alas, and the facade belies the interior in no small way.

Mr. James Day and Mr. Archie Lansdowne are two long-standing members of the Comrades Club. Mr. Lansdowne has been treasurer of the club for 30 years and will be remembered by many people as the Manager of the Home and Colonial Stores when it was in King Street.

Mr. Day, a past-president and secretary, and committee member for eight years is now part of the committee in charge of the house and garden, and together with Mr. Lansdowne, showed me round the club, telling me the history at the same time.

At the end of the First World War, "Comrades Clubs" were

set up all over the country as social clubs for ex-servicemen and financed by profits from the NAAFI.

The first meeting of the Saffron Walden Branch was held in the Parish Room on March 18, 1918, and shortly after the club was formed it moved to Castle Street, and later to Dorset House in Church Street (now demolished).

Eventually No.55 High Street was purchased, the first meeting being held on the premises on March 20th 1930. Purely a male-orientated domain, it was only agreed to admit women about 20 years ago, and even now a woman can only become an associate member with no right to vote.

Although originally intended as a social club for ex-servicemen, membership is now open to all who wish to apply.

Like Gray Palmer's, DeBarr's Shoe Shop at No.50 has spanned the years and generations with an ease and confidence built up on a loyal customer relationship.

Behind the modern facade there exists almost 70 years of tradition and experience and three generations of personal involvement.

Still the original premises which young Walter DeBarr opened when he was invalided out of the army in 1915, but many times altered and modernised, and now going through yet another phase of revitalisation by Mr. David DeBarr, grandson of the founder of the business.

Notwithstanding this, the foundations of the business will remain the same. Parents, who came as children, can still bring their children along, knowing that they will have the benefit of an assistant skilled in the art of fitting youngster's shoes as did their parents before them.

Standing in DeBarr's one day, I found it difficult to stifle a smile as I watched a fashion-conscious tot being gently and carefully guided by Mr. Douglas Jones, one of DeBarr's senior assistants, into accepting shoes which were suitable for her particular needs. Mother and grandmother looked on with complete confidence.

This particular scene, reminded me of a conversation with Mr. Walter DeBarr junior (David's father) a few years ago.

Reminiscing over the changes he had seen since he entered the business in 1932, he said that, at one time there had always been a special type of shoe which was a necessary part of a schoolchild's uniform, but all that has changed, including the children.

He continued: 'In those days one expected young girls of 14 to be rather difficult, demanding something rather more fashionable than what their mother's had in mind.

'But now, fashion awareness starts at about the age of nine, and little girls of that age can be very choosey indeed. And whereas boys never used to be at all fashion conscious, now 50 per cent of them are very much aware of the latest trends.'

But if children change, parents don't and tradition dies hard when it comes to having their offspring's shoes fitted by DeBarr's.

That is why parents who have long since left the area and are now living in far-flung places like Hong Kong or Canada, or even nearer, London or Cambridge, all make the pilgrimage back to the shop where THEY were first fitted with shoes.

But times change also, and a pair of working men's boots, made of all leather no longer cost 10s.11d (60p) as they did in 1915. Probably that self-same boot would cost nearer £40, but Mr. Walter DeBarr believes that modern technology has helped in no small way to keep the cost of shoes at a reasonable price level.

Next door to DeBarr's at Nos.52 and 54 we come to the first premises which Albert John Cole, the Baker, bought in the 1930s, and which he supplied from his Bakery in Great Chesterford, and which are still an important part of the A.J. Cole enterprise.

Across the road Nos.57 and 59 High Street are charming examples of early 18th century (57) and 17th century (59) houses. Whilst No.61 is a splendid specimen of Victorian Gothic architecture, designed by William Beck, an architect about whom little is known, except that he was the first architect to resign from the Royal Institute of British Architects in 1887.

His work was greatly influenced by Pugin, advocate of the Gothic revival. This in turn led to lesser local architects copying Beck's style resulting in a minor Gothic revival in Saffron Walden itself.

William Beck lies in the churchyard at nearby Strethall, but his lasting monuments are represented by the Hospital in London Road, and the house known as "The Vineyards" commissioned by William Tuke.

The Job Centre at No.62 will be remembered by many as Frank Bacon's fruit and fish shop. Older people will recall the days when it was The Clifton Hotel, an unpretentious boarding house run by Mrs. Fred Vert.

The gleaming cars in the showroom of Walden Motors are evidence of another family business.

Thirty-five year-old Charles Hobbs, assisted by his wife Margaret, carry on the business which Charles' father started in 1938. Which means, not just selling cars, but also continuing the family tradition of a caring after-sales service.

Managing Director, Mr. Maurice Hobbs says, 'I have very rarely lost a customer but on the isolated occasion this has happened, I have felt very hurt indeed.'

Although now semi-retired Mr. Hobbs still keeps his finger on the pulse of the business taking a keen interest in the enterprise he started with exactly £40.

A Somerset man by birth, Maurice Hobbs came to Saffron Walden at the age of 14 in 1927. For a number of years he worked for Crawley Agrimotors which later became Acrows before they moved out to Ashdon Road.

Although an engineer by profession, he preferred motor cycles to tractors and dragsaws, and became a keen grasstrack racer. It was also his love of motorbikes which helped him woo a pretty young hairdresser.

'I think I must have been a forward young hussy,' laughs Mrs. Hobbs, 'I used to see him riding up and down on his bike and I would call out after him – would you like to give me a ride on your motor-bike?'

Forward or not, young Frieda Walls gave Maurice the opportunity he was looking for, and he needed no persuading to give Miss Frieda a lift – as good a way as any to start a romance.

In 1938 Maurice Hobbs quit engineering to set up his own business in Station Road, repairing motor cycles and cars.

It was hard going, and he worked long hours, including weekends, but finally he had the satisfaction of owning a flourishing car showroom (now the showroom of Saffron Walden Building Supplies), petrol station and repair workshop.

In 1959 he bought Nos.64 and 66 High Street from Mr. Frank Bailey who had a garage and motor repairs workshop at the rear, and converted the premises into the showroom we know today.

In the 1920s No.64 was occupied by Mr. A.E. Kett, an electrician who gained a reputation for himself by fitting a loudspeaker into one of the windows above the shop and broadcasting the news on what was then the "new-fangled wireless".

Going back to the beginning of the century this building was an attractive plaster and timber-framed house belonging to John Hughes, a coachbuilder. But a fire in 1912, seriously damaged it, and it is believed that a brick-facade was added as part of the restoration.

Walk up the stairs of No.66a; turn sharp right and open the

The High St at the turn of the century

31

door in front of you. As you walk over the threshold you enter a forgotten age, irrevocably bound to the 20th century by the invisible bonds of craftsmanship and tradition.

Clocks, clocks, clocks and yet more clocks, ticking softly, gently and sometimes loudly; recording the passing minutes with ruthless persistence. Two men sit, bent over their work in loving concentration; they are Michael Eves and David Hopkins, members of the Guild of Clock and Watchmakers.

They belong to that rare breed who work, not simply just to earn a living, but for the satisfaction of a job well done.

Both Walden men born and bred; they learned their trade the hard way, but thoroughly and with competence.

Michael Eves started in the watch trade with Mr. Leonard Pitstow in 1944 in King Street, a shop which is now a Unisex hairdressers. Later he joined David Hopkins at James' the Jewellers, and like David, served his National Service as a watch-maker in the Army.

Later they both worked for Mr. Gatwood in Cross Street (now Derek Munday's) and when, after 20 years service the business was sold, they found themselves without a job.

But a craftsman is always a craftsman first and foremost and it would be unthinkable for such a man to enter any but his chosen profession. So Michael and David decided to set up on their own, starting off by acquiring contracts from various jewellers and working in their own homes.

Then they discovered that a room at No.66a overlooking the High Street was available, and with nothing else but the tools of their trade, they walked in and established their business. That was seven years ago.

They say they have never needed to advertise. Their customers come from far and wide, returning time and time again. And their work encompasses fine old grandfather clocks, tiny, exquisite ladies' watches, jewellery and small antiques.

'We have just moved into the quartz world,' Michael said with a sad shake of his head, 'but it is not very satisfying. You have to go along with the times though.'

No.67 High Street across the road is yet another pleasing example of early 18th century architecture, now belonging to a Group Practice of local doctors, Chalmers, Sills and Smith.

But a glance at the old rating lists of 1840 shows us that this has been a house and maltings at one time, owned by Wyatt George Gibson "and others".

Described in the lists as "house, counting-house, corn shops, stables, etc., and two malting offices" it must have been a considerable enterprise.

This was at the time Joshua Clarke lived there. Joshua was the youngest son of Turner Clarke, a farmer who lived at The Roos, near Debden.

In his youth Joshua was apprenticed to his Uncle, Charles Baron the shoe-maker, but later became a maltster in partnership with the Gibsons.

As a maltster he was extremely successful and became very wealthy. He took an active part in public life and was town councillor for 48 years, and Mayor 10 times. The present mayoral chain was one of his gifts to the town.

He also developed an interest in ornithology and bequeathed his collection of birds to the Museum on his death.

According to old rating lists No.69 High Street was built about 1884 as a Caretaker's House for the Friends' Meeting House which itself had been rebuilt in 1879.

It was built on the site of an old leather works, which first appears in the rating lists of 1790 as "house, barn stables and land" belonging to Erswells Charity – a Charity which owned similar property in various parts of the High Street.

At first it was rented by John Mallyon, and then later, in 1807 by William Nichols, a Currier. In 1869 the business passed from William to his son Charles, and then in 1864 to his grandson Henry.

In 1886 the word "empty" appears in the lists by the side of No.69, but in 1867 it had been purchased by George Stacey Gibson, remaining empty until 1870 when it is referred to as "schoolhouse" etc.

It is believed by some that this was probably the temporary site of the old Grammar School after its removal from Castle Street, before the new Grammar School was built in Ashdon Road in 1881.

As the last master of the Grammar School was the Rev. Alfred Enoch Fowler, who lived next door at No.67 from 1851 until the turn of the century, it seems quite feasible to suppose that the Grammar School was carried on in one of the barns belonging to No.69, a not unusual practice for those days, as barns were far more substantially built than their 20th century counterparts.

Some confusion in the rating lists does arise because of the Adult School started by the Friends soon after the Caretaker's House had been built, but which was housed in the actual building, and which continued until 1941, when it became the office of the Medical Officer of Health, and later the Health Services Clinic until sometime in the 70s.

No. 74 is the home of the wellknown local architect and former Mayor of Saffron Walden, Mr. Ian Wright-Watson, and his wife Tess.

By an odd co-incidence, No.74 was also the birthplace of the first lady mayor of Saffron Walden, Mrs. Joy Hawkins. Mr. Wright-Watson says that the house itself is about 400 years old, and that like Topsy, it has just "growed" over the centuries.

Next door to No.74 is Stocks Yard. An unexpected bonus of almost rustic charm. No.1 Stocks Yard is a picturesque cottage, restored by Ian Wright-Watson and now occupied by Mrs. Shirley Massingham, who told me there are three cottages in all, believed to have belonged to a maltings at the rear of the High Street.

But the rating lists of 1850 mention Hannah Stock who owned no less than three cottages adjacent to No.74 from whom we may suppose we get the name "Stocks Yard".

The Census lists for 1851 give us "Ann Stock, Washerwoman, retired." Assuming Ann Stock and Hannah Stock are the same person, it would appear that she had done quite well out of her humble profession.

No.71 High Street was once the home of yet another well-loved Saffron Walden doctor. In 1944, Dr.Hepworth, retired and terminally ill, was nursed by Margaret Anderson, a young woman filling in her time before taking her midwifery qualifications. (Later Margaret and her sister Kathleen were to become the town's first Queen's District Nurses).

She recalls the time when she was standing at the top of No.71, looking out of the window, when the Ammunition

Dump blew up in Chesterford Great Park, shaking the whole house from top to bottom.

It must have been at this very moment that Gladys Trigg, (a former young lady of Cambridge House School) found herself on the doorstep of No.72 High Street, the home of the Miss Claydens, those gentle ladies whose former house had been demolished to make way for the Co-op grocery store in 1934.

But not even the blowing up of a nearby ammunition dump could disturb the ordered, disciplined lives of the Miss Claydens, and Gladys Trigg was invited in, and whilst the rest of Saffron Walden panicked, afternoon tea, poured from a silver teapot, was served in the calm, unruffled atmosphere of the drawing room at No.72.

Incredible to think that, although the Quakers have influenced the development of Saffron Walden in no small way, their arrival in the town during the 17th century was far from welcome.

Persecuted and imprisoned, they continued to follow their chosen beliefs, despite the consequences, and met openly in private houses until a cottage in Cuckingstool End Street was purchased for £20 in 1676. This was the first Quaker Meeting House in Saffron Walden.

Their troubles were to last for many years after that; but they still continued to meet, and were later able to enlarge their Meeting House by the purchase of two more cottages.

Eventually, in 1879 the three cottages (next door to No.69) were pulled down to make way for the present Meeting House which is now a familiar and important part of the High Street scene today.

No.73, with its air of Regency elegance, cream-coloured stucco facade, fine six-panelled front door and Adamesque fanlight, is, according to records, probably a later 17th century or very early 18th century building.

And almost opposite No.73 stands all that remains of what was once a farm. Department of Environment records describe No.76A as an "18th century, probably earlier, timber-framed and plaster house". Rating lists for the year 1841 describe it as being part of "Erswells Charity, farmyard, barns and cottage." Later in 1850 "three unfinished houses".

dignified 18th century building – still standing – but sadly hidden from view by its 19th century successor. To have some idea of what the early "Upper Meeting" looked like, walk through the precinct of The Maltings, and look right, there one will see a sideways view of a splendid late Georgian building.

It was built in 1774, and became known as "The Upper Meeting" because the first non-conformist Meeting House in Saffron Walden was in Abbey Lane. But after a quarrel in 1774 when the Rev. Joseph Gwennap was "voted out of his pulpit" two deacons and most of the congregation left together with their pastor to worship in a barn belonging to Elizabeth Fuller, next door to her house in Myddylton Place. Here they continued to worship until their new meeting house was opened.

It was Elizabeth Fuller who provided the money to purchase the land in Bailey's Lane (Audley Road) and who also gave £400 toward the cost of building.

The later Church, built in 1879, was added to the west side of the original one, thus fronting the High Street, and the former building relegated to the role of Sunday School and Church functions.

From 1863 until shortly after the First World War a lamp post stood on the pavement in front of the Church. Originally this lamp stood in the middle of the Market Square and can often be seen on very old photographs of that part of town. It was replaced by a drinking fountain presented to the town by George Stacey Gibson and his mother to commemorate the marriage of the Prince of Wales (later King Edward VII) and removed to a position just outside the Baptist Church. Later it was moved again to make way for the War Memorial.

But it still stands, with twin lamps, converted from gas to electricity, on the pavement between Nos.89 and 90.

Hill House, somewhat diminished in splendour, enjoys a premier position at the top of the High Street. Once the home of George Stacey Gibson, it was originally built by Henry Archer in 1821.

George Stacey, son of Wyatt George Gibson, bought No. 75 High Street in 1845 after his marriage to Elizabeth Tuke, daughter of Samuel Tuke, a rich tea merchant from York.

Shortly after he acquired the property he enlarged it, extending the grounds, which stretched as far as the Battle Ditches, to link up with the gardens of his father's house at No.53.

Sadly, the back of the house faces the street, and we do not see the highly ornate but still beautiful "Italian Villa" facade which once looked out onto sweeping green lawns, now reduced to a few meagre yards and a car park.

George Stacey Gibson was perhaps the best loved and remembered of all the Gibsons. It was he who funded the removal of the Friends' School from Croydon to Saffron Walden; founded the Teacher-training College (now the International College); enlarged the Town Hall, and built an additional wing to the almshouses.

He was also a keen botanist and wrote "Flora of Essex" a major standard work on the subject.

George Stacey Gibson died in 1883 at the age of 63, without male issue, and only one daughter, Miss Mary Gibson, who never married and died at the age of 77 in 1934. The late Stanley Wilson, in his book "Saffron Crocus", writes that generations of servants declared the house haunted by the ghost of a girl of 19.

Nelly Ketteridge, an under-housemaid employed by the previous owner, Mr. Archer, was walking from Saffron Walden to her home in Elmdon one bitterly cold January day in 1845, when she was caught in a terrible snowstorm. Six weeks later her body was found in a ditch. Now, it is said her spirit walks the corridors and bedrooms of Hill House followed by an icy-cold draught! And Mr. Wilson assures his readers that many visitors to Hill House left rather hurriedly after spending only one night under its roof!

After the death of Miss Gibson, Hill House, once so elegant and gracious, started to decline. It was taken over by the Military Authorities during the war, and later became the G.P.O. Sorting Office, and the splendid gardens sold as building land.

Within the last few years Hill House has again changed hands, and is now owned by the Baptist Housing Association, a non-profit making body specialising in buying and converting large old houses and mansions into flats and dwellings.

Hill House stands on the corner of what we know as Margaret Way. It was here that the "Cucking Pond" was situated, thus giving its name to this part of the High Street – "Cuckingstool End Street", a name which survived until 1825 when it was changed to "High Street."

The term "end" sometimes refers to a certain quarter or part of a town. And the term "cucking-stool" refers to the actual stool used to duck (or chuck) sharp-tongued ladies into the pond as a means of punishment. (Cuck being a corruption of chuck). So the women were literally "chucked into the water!"

The cucking or ducking pond was a feature of every town and village throughout the country for centuries, and was still in existence in Saffron Walden as late as 1829; part of it becoming the lily pond in George Stacey Gibson's garden.

For another Ghost story we cross the road to another modern block of flats, built at an angle to the High Street - Ingleside Court.

The story goes thus: "One of the first tenants in these flats was a young teacher, who was wakened from her slumber one night when an old man, carrying a scythe entered her room and asked if she wanted anyone to work in her garden. When she told him she didn't have a garden, he thanked her and went away.

Only afterwards did she realise how strange it was, and wondered how he had managed to get into her room. On making enquiries from another tenant, who had known the old house which once stood on the site of the flats, she realised her description tallied with that of an old gardener who had worked at Ingleside House for many years."

Ingleside House will be remembered as the Headquarters of the local Territorials and the Recruiting Office and Headquarters of the Local Defence Volunteers during the First World War.

Later it became the home of Mr. Edward Trew, the Tallyman when he moved from No.62. Mr. Trew sent his employees out with large suitcases filled with ladies' and children's clothes. And poor people, who could not afford to buy new clothes outright, bought first and payed later – a few pennies or shillings a week to Mr. Trew's salesmen.

Edward Trew's widow later sold the house to Mr. Deasey Dix the antique dealer. Deasey Dix was a great local character whose real name was Arthur, but who acquired his extraordinary nickname when he attended the local Grammar School. (Deasey being a corruption of the French word for 10 – dix!)

Nos. 88, 89, 90 and 92 were once called Ingleside Terrace, now they are all part of the High Street.

They are recorded as being "a 17th century timber-frame and plaster house, completely refronted in the late 19th century, still showing the form of medieval houses with a long frontage, the end gables jettied in the first storey."

This is believed to have been an Inn called The White Hart (not to be confused with The White Hart where Cambridge House now stands) which was purchased by the Churchwardens and Vestry in 1734 for the first-ever recorded Workhouse in Walden.

Later, in 1818, the Gaol was removed from the Town Hall in the Market Place and erected next door to the Workhouse, so that the destitute and the guilty worked side by side.

Between Nos. 92 and 94 there was a small alley leading to Ingleside Place, known as Albert Place. One of the many tiny communities in the town which were demolished just before the Second World War under a slum clearance act.

The Duke of York is an early 19th century public house, built on land, if my records are correct, which probably contained a group of small cottages or barns belonging to a farm sited here in the 18th century.

It was here that I met Pete and Marian Lancaster, joint licensees of The Duke of York for the past 16 years. When I spoke to them in the Spring of 1984 they said they thought it would be a big year for the Duke of York, their Brewers were about to repay the loyalty of their customers by installing inside lavatories.

'The lavatories are right out at the back,' said Pete, 'and the customers have to tramp through snow, ice, howling gales and pouring rain to get to them. How they have put up with it I shall never know. It is simply that they are marvellous people and have never complained!'

No.77 High Street, known as The Gables, is one of those

41

Saffron Walden houses photographed, painted and sketched time and time again. Originally a 16th century timber-framed building, in the 18th century a second wing was added, the whole building refaced and the highly ornate pendent barge-boards added.

According to the old rating lists James Searle, the Banker, set up a maltings on part of the land belonging to this house. But these were pulled down in 1825 at the time of the collapse of Searle's Bank.

From 1860 until the turn of the century, the Miss Blenkin-sops ran their preparatory school at The Gables, and it is alleged to have been said by an ex-pupil many years ago, that, 'the Miss Blenkinsop's knew very little, but they taught it very well!'

At No. 83 Elijah Levi the glove-maker lived with his family. Elijah died in 1830 at the age of 73, but his son James, then James' sister carried on the trade until she married in 1900 when her married sister took over, and as late as 1915, Stephen Acco, another member of the family was still making gloves at these same premises.

We now come to Barnards' Court, a delightful experience in itself. A tiny cluster of small cottages once belonging to Barnard Brothers Coal Depot, which have been thankfully left to survive the great urban improvement schemes of the 30s.

No.1 Barnards' Court is one of three tall, narrow little houses, one room deep, three storeys high, with basements. Believed to have been weavers cottages at one time, there is however, no record of this in the old ratings lists.   It is now the weekend home of Mr. Joe Byrne and his wife Eileen, who both work for the social services in London. But many years ago Mr. White the basket-maker lived here.

Close by I found "Battle Cottage", a picturesque little house, so named because of its nearness to the Battle Ditches.

Now we follow the curve of the road, from The Duke of York to Debden Road. It was here, during the latter part of the 18th century that there stood a strangely macabre phenome-non – a wall, 7ft high, made entirely of animal bones. Who innovated this curiosity no-one seems to know, but it is said that the bones were collected from local butchers.

Fortunately it had a comparatively short life, and by 1820

had deteriorated so much it was demolished and the ground it stood upon, used for building purposes.

We have now reached the top of the High Street and the houses begin to melt into London Road and Saffron Walden itself spreads outwards toward the green fields.

It was here sometime during the 15th century that the Saffron crocus grew - the tiny flower which brought prosperity to the town and is perpetuated in the name.

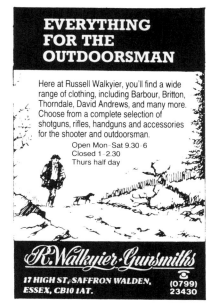

EVERYTHING FOR THE OUTDOORSMAN

Here at Russell Walkyier, you'll find a wide range of clothing, including Barbour, Britton, Thorndale, David Andrews, and many more. Choose from a complete selection of shotguns, rifles, handguns and accessories for the shooter and outdoorsman.

Open Mon-Sat 9.30-6
Closed 1-2.30
Thurs half day

R.Walkyier-Gunsmiths

17 HIGH ST, SAFFRON WALDEN, ESSEX, CB10 1AT.

(0799) 23430

COLE'S
Traditional Bakery Ltd
EST. 1939

SPECIALISTS IN OUTSIDE CATERING

We are able to offer a complete package for your
CATERING REQUIREMENTS.

We supply marquees, food, wines, spirits, champagne, flower arrangements, we organise photography and toastmasters.

Personal advice and experienced planning to make your function a success.

COLES TRADITIONAL BAKERY LTD, London Road, Great Chesterford
Saffron Walden, Essex CB10 1PG   Tel: (0799) 31053 Fax (0799) 31140

HAMPTONS

AUCTIONEERS ESTATE AGENTS
VALUERS SURVEYORS
AUCTIONEERS OF FINE ART
AND ANTIQUES
AGRICULTURAL AUCTIONEERS
AND VALUERS

The agents with an unrivalled knowledge of North West Essex. We know the properties, the people, the villages and the problems.

Gibson House, Market Hill, Saffron Walden, Essex
(0799) 22628
Please contact Bruce Munro FSVA
or Michael J Snow BSc FRICS CAAV

Head Office: 6 Arlington Street, St. James's, London SW1A 1RB

44

CHAPTER TWO

Freshwell Street

First published in the Saffron Walden Weekly News
June 7–14 1984

Standing in Freshwell Street on a warm Spring morning, with the noise of the birds in the background, and the quacking of the ducks on New Pond, I felt the centuries slip gently away. I might have been standing in a village street one, two, perhaps three hundred years ago.

Charm, peace and tranquility enveloped me until, suddenly I was almost squashed to a pulp against the wall of a nearby cottage as an enormous lorry thundered by. I knew I was back in the 20th century.

Not to be aware of Freshwell Street and New Pond is to forego the pleasure of experiencing the last piece of rural Walden. And yet, this tiny, narrow lane, just off Bridge Street, can so easily be missed unless you are aware of its existence.

In her Thesis on Saffron Walden, Mrs. Monteith says, the curve of the street probably owes its shape to the wooden palisade which protected the first Saxon village. It would, of course, have been an important part of the village because of the abundance of water from the nearby springs.

Whilst Mr. H.C. Stacey, writing in the Saffron Walden Antiquarian Society's Journal, October 1972 says: "in the 14th and 15th centuries there was a Fullerstret on the western edge of town, near to the springs, presumably used by the fullers (bleachers of cloth)." He continues to say that in a deed of 1437 the name Frosshwell Hundred appears, later to be called Freshwell Hundred.

In the 18th century Freshwell Hundred became Horn Lane, this name appears in the old rating lists for 1575.

Again, referring to Mrs. Monteith's Thesis, it was the bone

wall, which stood behind Freshwell House, which was responsible for the change of name. The wall, composed of bones and horns of cattle, like the one which stood at the top of the High Street, was all part of the old Tannery which stood somewhere on this site. And as this was in the days before bonemeal became a useful form of fertilizer, probably these walls were more common than is generally supposed.

The first recorded evidence of the Tannery is in 1794 when Joseph Collin owned a house, Tan Office and meadow somewhere near here. As Freshwell House dates back to the 16th century in parts, and the bone wall was built behind these premises, it is not unreasonable to assume that this was the actual nucleus of the Tannery.

By 1796 Joseph Collin was dead, and the whole complex owned by Thomas Smith.

In a letter in the Town Library files, written by a Mr. Reuben Heffer of Gold Street, and dated October 1913, he mentions the bone wall "which existed until quite recent date at the back of Mr. Hutchesons (Freshwell House). The Tannery being close by the old barn which still stands in Freshwell Street, near Bridge Street."

Between Nos. 6 and 8 there is what appears to be an old barn, and notes in the Town Library state that: "there was a Tannery at Williams' (No14) in Horn Lane. Next to Williams' house was a large shed with an open lattice window in which the hides were hung to dry after going through the vats. There were tan vats in the yard as well as large blocks of Yorkshire stone to beat the hides on. The owner was known as Tanner Smith."

Department of Environment records say that Nos. 2 to 8, the barn, Freshwell House and No. 14 are all part of one group of buildings. This again would appear to support the theory that this was the site of the old Tannery.

Tanner Smith, lived to the ripe old age of ninety, according to Reuben Heffer. He became a J.P. and a man of substance (Tanners usually were because leather was such a useful and important commodity).

Reuben Heffer, who was himself born in 1833, says that his grandfather worked for Thomas Smith for 54 years, so he must have been with him right from the start.

But by 1857 the Tannery was no longer in existence. It had passed into the hands of John Dickinson Jackson in 1849, who rented it from Jonathon Bennett, but eight years later it is described as "empty".

By 1871 Horn Lane had become Freshwell Street, apart from a group of small cottages further down the street near the pond. These were to continue to be called Horn Lane until 1873, when they became known as Jones Yard, after Edgar Jones who bought them.

From the gracious exterior of Freshwell House (formerly known as "The Saffrons"), it is difficult to imagine it as part of an old Tannery. And walking up the gravel pathway to the meadow behind the house, where probably the tan vats stood, no evidence of the grisly bone wall can be seen.

Although Freshwell House itself dates back to the 16th and early 17th centuries, with later 18th century alterations, it presents a curiously modern facade for such an old building. On the left hand wall of the house however, some fine examples of original old pargetting can be found.

Many people will remember that Freshwell House played its part in the Second World War by providing accommodation for the girls of Tottenham High School. An entry in the school's "Evacuation Magazine for 1940" under the heading "Surprises" written by Eileen Brabant of form VL, gives an amusing account of the girls' first impression of Saffron Walden.

She says, "the weather here is a never-failing source of surprise to us. In no other place does it seem to rain as hard or as long". After a few more lines in similar vein she finishes her paragraph by saying "To enjoy oneself in Saffron Walden, it is necessary to be equipped with a large mackintosh, an even larger umbrella, and rubber boots reaching to the knees." (Oh come now Miss Brabant!)

She then continues, "the actual town of Saffron Walden surprised us, as we were expecting to find ourselves in a village with only one shop, and we could hardly contain ourselves when we discovered a cinema and a row of shops!"

No. 14 Freshwell Street has an air of solid 19th century red-brick respectability. A fitting house for Richard Atkinson Williams, Jobmaster!

W.A. Williams appears on the scene as tenant of John Kettle in 1873, owner of the house and premises (once part of the Tannery). But by 1886 Richard Atkinson Williams owns the property and is a firmly established entrepreneur in Freshwell Street.

Oil merchant, glass and china dealer and manufacturer of aerated waters, he was the sole licensee in the district for "Zoedone". Zoedone being, according to the advertisement in the Town Almanack – "an extremely agreeable, refreshing and invigorating beverage with important recommendations!"

By 1896 Williams' Livery Stables are playing the most important role in the life of Freshwell Street. He is now advertising "vehicles let out by the hour or day. Saddle

No. 14 once part of a tannery

horses; reliable coachmen; shooting parties arranged on lowest terms" (presumably the transport not the marksmen). And oh, joy of joys! "A handsome new hearse, prepared to undertake funerals, distance no object!"

Later the Almanack for 1914 shows R.A. Williams in partnership with S.M. Segers, Job and Livery Stables, and also Motor and Engineering Works and Garage. They still advertise carriages of every description, but now also "open and closed motor cars for hire," and "experienced drivers" have replaced the "reliable coachmen!"

By this time the aerated water side of the business must have been sold to Robson & Sons, who were advertising their manufacturery in Freshwell Street in the town Almanack for 1903.

But now there is no trace left of the old Livery Stables, just a cluster of modern houses, eliminating for all times evidence of a slower, more relaxed way of living than ours.

The latter part of the 19th century and the early decades of the 20th found Freshwell Street an important and thriving community in Walden.

The actual premises of the people who carried on their small businesses are difficult to locate however. At No. 13 for instance for many years Fanny Edwards the dressmaker lived, but where was No. 13? And No. 3 was the home of William Rush, the gardener, but I have searched in vain for the house of J.T. Frye, Professor of Music. Nor can I discover where Miss Ewin kept her small general shop, or where Mrs Smith the Launderess lived. But they were all there in 1886, playing their role in the life of the communtiy.

——— · ———

Jones Yard or Freshwell Gardens as it is now known has its own sad tale to tell.

All that is left of the original group of old cottages which once formed an essential part of Freshwell Street, is a fine old Tudor House called Fearns. This is the home of Mrs. Norah Barham who came to Freshwell Street sixteen years ago from Rickling Green.

49

Mrs. Barham showed me over her lovely house which she and her husband bought as three semi-derelict cottages in 1968. It was the far-sightedness of Mrs. Hunter, the wife of the Museum Curator at that time, who saved the cottages from suffering the fate of the rest of Jones Yard. Left to crumble and slowly deteriorate, these picturesque old cottages were finally demolished and replaced by two rows of smart town houses facing Swan Meadow.

But Nos. 11, 12 and 13, believed to have been at one time an old Essex Hall House, were slowly and sympathetically restored to make a charming residence full of character and history. "Fearns" says Mrs. Barham is an old family name, and has nothing to do with the area.

Mrs. Barham's kitchen was Joe Byatt's cobblers' shop. Joe the cripple with one leg shorter than the other, walked with a broomstick for a crutch, and lived in Castle Street, but had No.1 for his workshop. In 1886 however, this must have been the workshop of Alfred Halls the boot and shoe-maker, who actually lived on the premises.

The enormous tie beam in one of the bedrooms at Fearns, and the massive timber construction of the house generally, would support the theory that Fearns was a Hall House and probably much older than records show.

I asked Mrs. Barham what she thought of the proposed use of Swan Meadow as a car park and she replied, 'where will they get in and where will they get out? It is so dangerous. They cannot even make it one way. And anyway, it is such a lovely spot in the heart of Walden, why not preserve it? They *cannot* take it away!'

No. 7 Freshwell Gardens is an attractive town house standing where once a simple cottage stood. It is the home of Mrs. Mamie Turner, who remembers Jones Yard when all the cottages were derelict. She has lived in Freshwell Gardens for fourteen years and says, 'it used to be so quiet, but now it has got busier and busier, and I originally chose the place because it was so lovely and peaceful.'

Mrs. Turner came from Gt. Chesterford soon after the death of her husband. She says, 'in Gt. Chesterford I used to have a lovely old horse called "Pride" peering at me over the garden fence. By a delightful co-incidence, soon after I arrived here,

Swan Meadow

so did Pride, in the meadow just the other side of the fence, and so we were able to keep up our friendship. If they turn the meadow into a car park, things like that just won't happen any more.

'And anyway, the pond is a lovely place for families to come and feed the ducks. They musn't make it into a car park!'

I made my way to the pond. Two middle-aged gentlemen were feeding the ducks, and the ducks were responding with the affability which ducks display whenever there is food around.

I asked Mr. Daniel Roberts of 23, DeBohun Court, what he thought about the prospect of Swan Meadow becoming a car park. He replied, 'as you see, we have just been feeding the ducks, and we fully intend to continue to feed the ducks. Do they realise it is called Freshwell because it floods? We have been told it can get up to three feet deep in very wet weather!'

The other gentleman, Mr. John Marshall, was Mr. Roberts' Australian cousin, on holiday in Britain for a few weeks. I asked him the same question, a look of horror spread over his

51

sunburned countenance. 'What! Cover all this with con-crete?' He surveyed the tangled, lush greenness of the meadows beyond the pond. 'It's sacrilige! Good God!'

It has been said the pond was called New Pond, after the old Ducking Pond was finally drained in the early 1860's.

On the 17th century map of Saffron Walden "The Pond Yard Spring" is clearly marked and "Swanne Meadow" extends as far as the rear of the old Swanne Inn in the High Street where the G.P.O. now stands.

In 1845 Swan Meadow is recorded as belonging to Lord Braybrooke. Later, John Dickinson Jackson, who bought the Tannery in 1850 owned the meadow. Seven years later Swan Meadow is again in the possession of Lord Braybrooke. And so it goes on, the land passing backwards and forwards as individual fortunes waxed and waned until all that is left now are the small green fields and the pond we see today.

Some say the pond was ruined soon after the 1914-18 war, when a road was made round the outer side of it so that motor vehicles could drive through when necessary to connect with Freshwell Street or Park Lane.

Controversy continues to rage about Swan Meadow. There are those who would have this unsophisticated spot for a car park. And there are those who raise their hands in horror at the very thought of it.

I discovered Mr. Robert Hildage, enjoying the Spring sunshine in Freshwell Gardens one morning, and asked him what he thought about the idea. Mr Hildage, a painter and decorator, has lived in Saffron Walden since 1946, although he originally comes from Scotland.

His feelings about Swan Meadow were not quite as enthusiastic as some however.

'It's supposed to be picturesque,' he said with a disgusted look at the surrounding greenness. 'The best thing anyone could do with it would be to turn it into a car park!'

But Swan Meadow holds many pleasant memories for those who have lived in Walden all their lives. It was here, sometime in the early decades of this century that a fair was held in these very meadows. And it was here, that a certain Miss Edith Lacey, a London girl in service in Walden, met her future husband, an up and coming young butcher called Tom

Goddard. Edith and Tom were married in 1923, and their sons still run the family business in Church Street.

And it was here that a certain family called Harris, who used to travel around with the Fair, used to "pull-in" during the winter months. Later one of the sons, George, married a local girl –Elsie Jarvis – a young lady destined to play an important role in the life of the community.

Leaving the ducks and the pond and the greenness behind me, I walked slowly up Freshwell Street towards Bridge Street, stopping in front of a small brick doorway in a wall. Known as "The Monks' Doorway" the doorway is believed to date from the time of Edward III when the Abbey stood where Audley End Mansion now stands, and is said to have been used by the Monks walking from the Abbey to the Parish Church.

Opinions differ on this point however and there are some who believe that the actual walk, which extends from the southern end of No. 21 Freshwell Street to Park Lane, is not as old as the actual doorway itself. D. of E. records state that "the western side of the wall consists mainly of 16th century brick, with tile courses, stone and flint to the lower parts and 18th century capping."

Nos. 19 to 21 on the east side of the Street are a range of 19th century brick almshouses built in 1881 by George Stacey Gibson.

Knocking on the door of No. 19A   I was greeted by Mrs. Ada Maskell. Mrs. Maskell has lived at No. 19A for twelve years and told me that before she came to Freshwell Street, she had never known what it was to have a decent bathroom and an inside lavatory let alone central heating.

Mrs. Maskell is a widow, but her husband Bertie must still be remembered by many people in Walden as a wellknown football player who played in the town team during the twenties and thirties.

Ada comes from South Croydon, and went into service like so many girls did in those days, as soon as she left school. First she worked at a house in Gt. Sampford, and then later, as kitchen maid at the Grammar School in Ashdon Road.

But it was whilst working as housemaid for Mr. Allen, the manager of Barclays Bank in the Market Place, that she met her husband Bertie, who used to deliver the coal. They were married in the early thirties, and went to live in a cottage in Debden Road.

Mrs. Maskell loves her little house in Freshwell Street, and says it is so warm and cosy, but is amazed at the changes in Saffron Walden itself.

She says, 'when I first came it was such a nice little Market Town, and now it has grown so much, I don't know half the streets. When I was in Gt. Sampford we used to come into town in a Pony and Trap and I liked it just the way it was.'

Across the road from the almshouses stands No. 8, a delightful colour-washed cottage recorded as probably 16th or early 17th century, a timber-framed and plastered house with an 18th century front. This and Nos. 15 and 17 (now all one house) and dated back to the 18th century, add in no small way to the picturesque charm of Freshwell Street.

The trend is continued by the long range of jettied 17th century timber-framed cottages which form Nos. 3 and 5, and whose walls are decorated with good examples of old pargetting.

No. 1 is yet again another 18th century house, with jettied storeys and curved brackets. Although the gable at the eastern end is in Bridge Street, this house nevertheless makes another contribution to what is a comparatively unspoiled part of Saffron Walden with its own unique history.

TALENTS

(Hingston Shops)

ORIENTAL and

HANDCRAFTED

GIFTS

13 KING STREET,
SAFFRON WALDEN,   Tel. (0799) 28253

CHAPTER THREE

King Street

First published in the Saffron Walden Weekly News
June 28 – August 16 1984

In the early 17th century Market Lane (the original King Sreet) was a narrow turning off the High Street, leading into Market Place, up Market Hill and round into Market Street.

By 1840, Market Lane had become Market End Street, and the rest known simply as "Market End". But by 1851 Market End Street disappears from the records and King Street appears.

It is said, but there is no trace in the rating lists, that at the time of Queen Victoria's Accession (1838), King Street was called Queen Street, but after a year, reverted to King Street again.

Some believe that King Street gets its name from the original "King's Arms" and that an Inn of that name once stood somewhere on the northern side of the road. This would seem quite feasible because in 1734 the King's Arms in Market Hill was called "The Plow" and earlier still, "The Post Horse".

This theory is strengthened by the fact that D. of E. records state that Nos. 22 and 26 were originally a late 15th century house built on a half "H" shaped plan with wings extending north on either side of a waggon-way which still remains. This could have been the site of an old Inn. And if it *was* called the King's Arms (or Head) knowing that old habits die hard, it is quite possible that this particular part of the street was always referred to as "King Street".

Whatever the origins of its name however, King Street has certainly changed considerably throughout the centuries.

In the 18th century a whole row of small shops which stood

between Harts and Hardwick's, known as "le Draperie" was demolished. The only evidence of it having ever existed is the width of the road from Hepworths on the north side and Hardwicks on the south upwards towards the market. A row behind le Draperie, Creepmouse Alley, also suffered the same fate.

To be logical, we really ought to approach King Street from the High Street end, as that is where it really began. But it will be less confusing for us if we walk down King Street from Market Place towards the High Street and start at No. 1 Gray Cook, the Estate Agents.

Mr. Martin Walshe, residential Sales Manager at Gray Cook told me that Gray Cook came to Saffron Walden just over three years ago as a natural extension of their business in Cambridge and other parts of East Anglia.

However, fifty years ago, these smart, modern offices were a butcher's shop owned by Mr. P.E. Wedd, the Butcher. And a hundred years ago, this was where Henry Machon the Chemist had his shop.

Next door to Gray Cook stands the restrained Victorian Gothic splendour of Lloyds Bank, which was once, before the first World War "The Capital and Counties Bank".

Across the road stands a mid-19th century stuccoed building in what is termed as "a free classical style", and believed to have been designed by William Beck. And undoubtedly the Town Library and the adjoining Librarian's House (now James' the Jewellers) are certainly very handsome buildings.

The Town Library was known for over a 100 years as The Literary and Scientific Institute, but is now officially recognised as The Saffron Walden Town Library or The Victorian Studies Centre.

It was first set up in 1832 as an institution for working men's reading and mental improvement. However few working men in those days could afford even the very modest subscription fee, and the institution gradually became a middle-class subscription library.

By the end of the 19th century, the Literary and Scientific Institute had become so affluent that a resident Librarian was installed. But during the first World War, its fortunes declined and the house and Library were used by the army.

For a short time it enjoyed renewed popularity during the twenties and early thirties, dwindling once again with the coming of the County Library to the town. And eventually serious financial problems resulted in the Trustees renting the downstairs portion of the Librarian's house to a local jeweller.

Finally, in 1967, it was decided to hand the Library over to the County, with the proviso that all the books should remain in the original building, and that books must continue to be added to the collection.

At this juncture, the present Librarian, Mr. John Shaw-Ridler, was asked to establish a special study centre on the premises. This resulted in The Centre for Nineteenth

Booths, James the Jewellers (the Librarian's house) and the Library

Century Study being set up, the name gradually evolving into "The Victorian Studies Centre".

The establishment of the Centre co-incided with an upsurge in interest in Victoriana, and Mr. Shaw-Ridler felt that the nucleus of the collection should be art, antiques and architecture of this period. Also, because of the interest of one of the early founders (George Stacey Gibson) he decided there should also be a strong natural history section. It was his intention the interest should be forward rather than backwards, encompassing the first part of the twentieth century.

James the Jewellers is one of the town's longest established businesses. Its origins can be traced back as far as 1863, when William Rickman Jeffrey, watch and clock maker, had a house and shop at No. 8 King Street (now Rumbelows).

In 1871 he was succeeded by John James, whose earliest known advertisement appears in Harts Almanack for 1872.

Tinged with nostalgia these old advertisements may be, but they are also an interesting reflection of their age.

What widow would dream of wearing a mourning ring these days? How many of us possess a real silver thimble, let alone a gold seal and key. And when a golden tan is a much prized status symbol, what lady would use a parasol?

John James died in 1883 and was succeeded by his son-in-law Henry William Day, who, on his retirement in 1911 handed over the business to John's son, Arthur Francis.

But increased rent charges caused Arthur to move from No. 8 to 41 (now David's the hairdressers), where he remained until his death in 1932, when his widow, Annie Arabella James (nee Pitstow) continued to run the shop with her nephew Leonard Earnest Pitstow, as a limited company, until her death in 1953.

In 1958 Leonard moved the business – still known as A. James (Jewellers) Ltd. – to the Librarian's House at No. 4 King Street, where he continued trading until he retired in 1971.

The present Managing Director, Mr. Norman Brian Newman, C.M.B.H.I., joined the company in 1947, taking over the business when Leonard Pitstow retired, but continuing to trade under the name known and loved by generations of Saffron Walden inhabitants.

Mr. Newman is vice-chairman of the British Horological Institute, and both his sons, Howard and Graham, are themselves fully qualified horologists, engaged in running the business.

Besides selling beautiful jewellery and gifts, the Newmans specialise in the restoration of antique clocks, watches and barometers, and also maintains many church and turret clocks, including Ely Cathedral Clock.

And although we may smile at the early advertisement of Arthur James in 1872, Mr. Howard Newman says, in all seriousness, that many of the services and goods mentioned in that advertisement are still offered today by this traditional, old-established business.

Next door to the Librarian's House is a shop which for over a century has sold drapery and haberdashery.

In the first decade of this century, Charles Spurge rented No. 6 King Street from the previous owner, Eleazer Edwards, Berlin Wool Dealer, who had been in business on these premises since before 1886.

In 1946, Mr. and Mrs. Derek Booth bought the business from Mr. Spurge and continued to run the shop as one of those indispensable little High Street shops where a housewife could buy all she needed for herself and family in the way of household linens, sewing aids, underwear and clothing.

Throughout the years the Booths made few major alterations, apart from moving the brass "dressing-up"rails which hung over the counters for the display of overalls and scarves etc., and the cash desk, with its glass pigeon holes, which used to stand in the middle of the shop.

But within the last few years the shop has again changed hands when Mr. and Mrs. Booth retired, and although still run along much the same lines, the calm, unhurried atmosphere of a real old-fashioned draper's shop now seems to be missing.

The building itself is described by D. of E. records as "a mid 19th century stucco fronted building in a rich Baroque style."

Between the Baroque grandeur of Booths and the lofty 19th century Gothic of Rumbelows, Lime Tree Court offers a delightful retreat from the hustle and bustle of King Street.

This tiny collection of small shops with its own characteristic appeal has now become an essential part of the life of Saffron Walden.

Many people will remember Lime Tree Court as Lime Tree Passage, a shadowy recess off the main thoroughfare. A dusty, ghost-like commune of small businesses and professional offices. A backwater from a forgotten age.

Nothing now remains of those long-ago sad days. Lime Tree Court throbs with life; a bold venture by the Planners which has paid dividends.

At the entrance to Lime Tree Court is the supremely elegant Martin Gunn Interiors, whose premises were once The Saffron Walden Building and Benefit Society.

Beryl and Martin Gunn have brought their own special flair to Lime Tree Court, turning a mournful, depressing building into an exciting Interior Decorator's Shop filled with beautiful things.

Lime Tree House, tall, narrow and handsome, stands at the top of the passage leading to the Court. A house of great beauty in more ways than one – actually Sue Eaton's Beauty Salon – its graceful exterior is complemented by a refreshingly light and pleasing Adamesque interior.

Here on fine, warm days, it is fun to sit at the white painted tables on the terrace at the front of the house, drinking coffee and watching the rest of Saffron Walden go by.

Sue Eaton and her husband Tony, bought Lime Tree House in 1983. Sue says, 'we were lucky to find it. I must have walked by hundreds of times, but never noticed the place all the years I had my Salon at No. 34 King Street. Then one day, someone told me it was up for sale.'

'It had been a solicitor's office for a long time, and later, part of Cleales Motor Spares Department. And although it was a lovely old building it looked terribly neglected and slightly forbidding.'

Although they have made a lot of altertions, Sue and Tony, who have designed everything themselves, have also tried to preserve the best features wherever possible.

But if Lime Tree House is a house of beauty, it is also a house of mystery. Very little is known of its origins. Even the Department of Environment fails to actually date the place, saying merely that it must have had a second storey added, or have been refronted "at a later date."

It was built, or altered, according to records, about 1880, by a prominent, wealthy and much respected man in the town, who never actually lived in the house himself, but appears to have installed a Miss Mary Hull in the premises in 1881.

Who Mary Hull was no-one seems to know. But Lime Tree House was a very grand house for a single lady to rent, if in fact she did *rent* it. Especially at a time when single ladies of means, seldom left the parental home, or, if in reduced circumstances, set up a school or small business, such as millinery.

Mary Hull does not appear to be related to anyone in the town. And later, she ended her days in Mount Pleasant Road.

The house itself, although beautifully proportioned in many ways, is only one room deep, with a completely blank wall at the back, apart from two small windows low down, and an underground passage (bricked up) under the cellars leading towards King Street.

Why is there so little known about Lime Tree House?

As the Victorian era was notorious for its hypocrisy (even in Saffron Walden) dare we suggest that, Lime Tree House, or whatever it was called in those days, was something other than respectable?

Leaving Lime Tree House we now turn left into the actual Court itself. Once stables and gardens stood on this site, later a warehouse. Now there are six small shops in a tiny covered-in precinct which leads into Church Street.

It would be best if we approach the shops as we come to them rather than in numerical order. And the first shop we come to is Susannah Bland's Cookshop.

Susannah, a Cordon Bleu Cook, had been living in London working as a Director's lunch cook before she decided to take the plunge and open the Cookshop, despite the fact that she knew nothing whatever about shop-keeping. But she felt she knew practically everything there was to know about cooking and cook-ware, and the sort of thing which housewives and other girls who cook for directors, are looking for, which accounts for the success of her business.

Next door to the Cookshop is Renoir, a small, exclusive shoe shop run by Denise Adams for Mr. and Mrs. Peter Webber.

Bill and Jean Southern at No. 1 Lime Tree Court need no introduction to all who know Saffron Walden well.

For over forty years the Southerns have been selling sweets and tobacco in Saffron Walden. And although times have changed, and Bill and Jean have adapted their business accordingly, their old-fashioned standards of courtesy and caring personalised service have never altered.

Bill Southern was born in St. Helens, Lancashire, but his family had close relatives farming in Hatfield Broad Oak. It was whilst visiting them in 1938 that Bill's father, an engineer, happened to go into a tobacconist's shop in Bishop's Stortford.

'This,' he said to the proprietor, 'is just the sort of little business that I would like.'

'There's one going in Saffron Walden,' the shopkeeper replied. 'It is not on the market yet, but I know Mrs. Green is wanting to sell!'

'And that,' says Bill, 'was how my father came to buy No. 11 King Street, which is now part of Hardwick's fish shop. It was a real oldy-worldy tobacconists' shop in those days, and we used to weigh out and make-up individual blends of tobacco for our customers.'

During the war Bill was in the Navy. And it was because of the war that Jean, came to live with her grandparents, who farmed the land next to Bill's uncle, and that is how Bill and Jean met!

When Bill came out of the Navy in 1947, they bought No. 13 King Street, and then later opened another shop further down the street for gifts, but finally decided that running two shops close together was uneconomical, so they moved everything into one shop.

Bill continues the story, 'we were at Nos. 37 and 39 King Street for about twelve years, and then Lime Tree Court opened-up and we felt it was a unique opportunity not to be missed.

'It is true that things have changed a lot since the old days, and we no longer weigh out tobacco, but just pass packets over the counter. But we still weigh out rather rich and fattening sweets and chocolates!'

Malcolm and Deborah Lay are at No. 2 Lime Tree Court. And although the service they offer is new and perhaps a little unusual for Saffron Walden, it is nevertheless very much in keeping with the character of the town.

Specialists in tea and coffee, they offer their customers over 80 different varieties of tea, and are happy to blend tea or coffee for individual tastes and palates.

Malcolm was a professional tea-taster for eighteen years; four of those spent with Twinings and the rest working for a Tea Broker in the City.

His job with the Tea Broker meant travelling to India several times a year; visiting plantations; looking at different methods of manufacture; tasting the tea and assessing whether it was suitable for the London market.

'You do not need to have a special palate,' says Malcolm, 'to become a professional tea-taster, it is simply a matter of practice. I used to taste between four and six hundred teas a day sometimes,' he continues, 'but I still enjoy a nice cup of tea.'

Deborah, an ex-air stewardess with Laker Airways, met Malcolm, who is a professional Highland Dancer, as well as being an expert on tea, when he danced for The British Caledonian Airways team.

When Laker Airways folded, they felt there was nothing to keep them South of the River, and they just happened to visit Saffron Walden one day, fell in love with the town, and saw a cottage in Castle Street they liked. 'Then we saw the shop, and that,' says Deborah, 'was it. Now we couldn't imagine living anywhere else!'

Roadshow Records and Tapes at No. 3 is another husband and wife enterprise. Graham and Steph Harding are already well known in the area, although they have actually only been in the retail business three years.

And it was because a local record dealer was closing down his business, and they desperately needed singles for their Roadshows, that Graham and Steph started selling records, first in the Town Hall, later in the Market on Saturdays.

After two successful years they decided to open-up a shop

which would enable them to offer a wider range of tapes and discs at competitive prices.

Besides running a successful records business and two highly popular Roadshows, Graham is also a qualified architect with his own practice locally.

Steph who comes from Kent, was an occupational therapist at the Ida Darwin Hospital in Cambridge before she entered the business full time.

Also helping to keep the business on the move is 24 year-old Steve Double from Ashdon. Steve also worked at the Ida Darwin Hospital as a recreation officer. He, like Graham and Steph feels that there is a lot going for the leisure industry these days because of the employment situation.

'People will be working less hours,' he says, 'and we are making provision for this.'

No 4 Lime Tree Court is David Mansfield's electrical spares shop where David not only sells spares but also repairs electrical and domestic appliances.

David was born in Church Street and went to the Boys' British School in Saffron Walden. When he left school he became an apprentice with the County of London Electricity Supply Company in the High Street – later to become Eastern Electricity. After leaving Eastern Electricity in 1972 he had a short spell with a local electrical firm before starting up his own business.

Leaving Lime Tree Court now and returning to King Street we cross over the road to discover yet another old established family business – Harts the Booksellers and Stationers.

This business has been associated with King Street for most of its long life. They have however, only been at No. 5 since May 1976, although the original business was first established at No. 21 (now Williams the Opticians).

Henry Hart was the son of a Linton carpenter, who, at the age of 13 was apprenticed to George Youngman, a Saffron Walden printer who owned the very first printing press in town.

His Indenture of Apprenticeship, written in beautiful copperplate handwriting on parchment, is still in possession of Hart-Talbot, the printers, today.

It guaranteed young Henry 'a wage of nine shillings per

week' for the duration of the term of his apprenticeship providing he 'did not commit fornication, contract matrimony, or haunt taverns or playhouses...'

Henry must have been an exemplary youth – or clever, and eventually qualified as a printer. It is believed that he worked for Youngman until he was 35, and then set up in business on his own account in 1836, in an old cottage behind the premises now occupied by Chew & Osborne's. Also, about this time, he opened a stationery shop on the other side of the street at No. 21.

The business flourished, and in 1865 he bought the double-fronted shop (now two shops, Olivers and Peter Dominic) with a large walled garden and outbuildings at the rear. Here he built a new printing works.

Henry died at the age of 82, to be succeeded by his son, William (the 'son' of Hart & Son) who was in turn succeeded by his son – Ernest).

Ernest Hart in his lifetime became a prominent member of

Henry Hart's grandson Ernest (seated centre) with employees of the old King Street printing works

the community; a pillar of the Congregational Church, a staunch and active Liberal, and an Alderman of the Borough Council.

Someone who remembers him well is 77 year-old Mr. Ralph Housden.

Mr. Housden was born at No. 7 Ashdon Road and went to Ernest Hart's printing works as soon as he left the Boys' British School in 1922 at the age of 14.

'I started as a machine hand,' he says. 'That means I worked a machine which was operated by a pedal. Another of my jobs was turning a huge flywheel which operated a larger machine. It was like a big traction engine, far too big for a boy to turn for more than half an hour at a time. So it took 2 boys to operate it in turns.

'Another machine which I operated was a hand-press, which is now in the Saffron Walden Museum.'

'That machine, was Henry Hart's original printing machine when he first set up in business!'

Ernest Hart did not believe in taking boys on as apprentices. He would say, 'if you are a good enough chap you will be kept on, and it will be up to you to see what you make of it.'

Nor did he believe in high wages, and for the first four weeks of Ralph Housden's working life he took home the magnificent sum of 2/6d (12p) a week.

'But,' he says, 'my father said if I wasn't earning more than that, I was to leave because it was not keeping me in shoe leather. So Ernest Hart put my wages up to 5/- (25p) and I stayed. After that I used to get 1/- (5p) rise every year.'

Young Ralph soon tired of working the machines and was transferred to the Composing Department. From then onwards he remained a compositor all his life, apart from a short break during the second World War, when he was directed to work of National Importance.

He recalls Ernest Hart as basically a very hard man.

'Although,' says Mr. Housden – who has been a prominent member of St. Mary's Church since the age of eight when he first joined the choir – 'if I wanted to go on a Choir outing, he never refused me, because he was a great Church man himself. Just as when, one of the men – a good cricketer – wanted time off to play in a cricket match, he never refused him either. Because, he was also very interested in cricket.'

Working conditions were pretty strict at Henry Hart's. Not an unusual thing for those days. And like many places the men were not allowed a mid-morning break. Fortunately Ernest Hart had a habit of never closing a door, just letting it bang back; so when the men were having their illicit mid-morning snack, they had fair warning of the approach of their boss.

The only holidays the men were allowed were Bank Holidays and one week in summer, taken without pay, which was compulsory.

A visitor to the printing works would usually be met by a flurry of chickens, a fierce old rooster, a couple of pigs and a pony. The pony was used to pull the cart which carried the pianos hired out to various halls and social occasions. (A piano in the 1920s was still something of a status symbol).

The man who looked after the pony and cart also looked after the other livestock, for the Harts lived over the shop, and like many people at that time were as self-sufficient as they could be when it came to food.

Ernest Hart died in 1930, leaving his two daughters, Margaret and Barbara, to cope with a badly neglected run-down business, the result of their father's energies being channelled into public, rather than business affairs.

They struggled on until 1932. And then a young printer from London, Edwin Turnbull, was brought in as a manager, to regenerate the declining business, and eventually he bought the company in 1934.

Edwin had married a young Saffron Walden schoolteacher, Daisy Maggs, a daughter of John Maggs, senior clerk in the office of Adams and Land, solicitors of Church Street.

Edwin and Daisy put all their youthful enthusiasm into reviving the business which Henry Hart had founded almost a hundred years before.

The young Turnbulls had five children altogether, includ-ing two sets of twins! Unhappily, the first pair of twins died when they were only a few months old, but the second pair, Angus and Mary, and their elder brother Jack, live on.

In the early days before Edwin took over, Harts not only sold books and stationery, but also an amazing assortment of fancy goods and a wide range of musical instruments as well.

'Even today,' says Mr. Angus Turnbull, 'there are quite a few pianos to be found in Saffron Walden inscribed with the name "Hart & Son".

The enormous range of goods, stocked by Harts, reflected the times when people relied more on local shops than they do now. And even as late as 1910 Hart & Son were advertising perfume, handbags and glove-boxes, as well as those framed texts, beloved of the Victorians, reminding all sinners of the terrible fate awaiting them in the next world!

'As the Turnbull children grew up they were gradually brought into the business. Angus Turnbull says he can never remember a time when he was not helping in the shop in some small way.

He and his brother Jack, would be at Saffron Walden Station by six òclock every morning, loading newspapers on to a handbarrow, 'then' he chuckles, 'we would roar down Gold Street in order to get up enough speed to cut up Cross Street! And before we went to school, all the newspapers would have been delivered.

'During the war,' (the Second World War), he says, 'we never missed a day without delivering the papers, and despite the fact that they might be covered in mud and blood from the Blitz, they always reached their destination.'

By this time Jack, who had been formally apprenticed to the Printing Trade in 1935, and entered the family printing works straight after he qualified, was an Ambulance Driver in London's Dockland.

Later, in 1944, Angus was also called-up and went into the Guards. Returning from the War in 1946, he also entered the printing side of the business.

Edwin Turnbull died in 1958, and Jack became Managing Director of the company.

In 1963 the family sold the double-fronted shop, and moved to the original premises of George Youngman, on the corner of Market Square and Market Street (now the wool shop).

Angus took over the management of the retail shop 'as a temporary measure,' 'and' he says, 'I have been temporarily managing it ever since!'

No. 1 however, proved to be too small for both stationery

and books and a separate establishment was opened next door to the Rose & Crown, purely for the sale of books.

During the tragic fire at the Rose & Crown on the night of 26th December 1969, Harts Bookshop was also damaged and over 5,000 books were lost in the fire.

Eventually, in May 1976 Harts acquired No. 5 King Street which enabled them to get all their departments under one roof. Later, they opened further premises in Church Street as an office equipment centre, managed by the Turnbull's eldest son, Martin.

Looking back over the years, Angus Turnbull says he is not sorry he entered the retail side of the business instead of becoming a Printer, but stresses that the success of the concern could never have been achieved without the support of Iris, his wife, who is – simply marvellous – and always ready to help in anyway possible at a moment's notice!

'No story about Harts would be complete though,' he continues, 'without mentioning an extremely well-loved member of the staff who worked for us from the age of 14 until she retired after over 50 years service. Miss Eva Turner will be remembered by a lot of people in the town, and will certainly not be forgotten by us.'

Whilst Angus was managing the retail shops, Jack had the responsibility of the Printing Works – still housed in the yard through the archway in King Street.

Apart from being extended, first in 1931 and later in 1936 to celebrate the firm's centenary, very little outward change occurred in the Printing Works.

During all this time, Ralph Housden, still worked upstairs in the Composing Room setting the individual letters of type by hand.

He was now a married man, having married a young Sunday School teacher, Gladys Auger, whom he had met whilst teaching at St. Mary's Sunday School. Gladys taught the girls, and Ralph the boys!

'Working conditions at the printing works,' says Mr. Housden, 'although far better than in the days of Ernest Hart, were very cramped at King Street. You could not turn round without bumping into somebody.'

Eventually in 1965, the volume of business had increased

so considerably it was decided to move to the new Shire Hill Industrial Estate.

'Things were much better at Shire Hill,' Ralph Housden continues, 'it was a much larger place. But it was terribly cold because at first there was no means of heating the building. Later they installed Calor Gas heaters.'

Gradually the printing division and the retail shops became operationally independent, and it was finally decided in 1977 that the business should be divided into two separate entities. The retail shops continued to trade under the name of W. Hart & Son (later to become just 'Harts') controlled by Angus Turnbull, and the printing side became Hart-Talbot Printers Ltd.

Before Harts took over No. 5 King Street however, it formed part of Boots the Chemists (together with No. 7) and earlier still it will be remembered as 'The Victorian Cafe' (later to become The Copper Kettle), a small bakers and confectioners run by the Taylor family who came into the town around the turn of the century.

The Taylors had four children, two boys and two girls, and during the first World War, one of the daughters married a young army officer named Ford Ennals. They had three boys, one of whom, is now the wellknown socialist MP. Mr. David Ennals.

The cafe part of the confectionery was upstairs at the back. And it was here, in the early 20s that three lady lecturers from the Teachers' Training College (Miss Frood, Miss Mack and Miss Chart) the late Stanley Wilson and Bill Harvey (who later married Miss Chart) met to discuss their ideas on socialism.

As we learned earlier, No. 7 formed part of Boots, now it belongs to January's the Estate Agents whose Manager, Mr. Geoff White – twin brother to the Town Clerk – came to Saffron Walden in 1968 from Enfield.

Across the road from January's stands an imposing example of 19th century Gothic redevelopment. Rumbelows, W.H. Smith, Godfreys, Stead & Simpson and Dewhursts, all enjoy the lofty red-brick splendour of the late Victorian era.

Not all that long ago, Cleales Motor Engineers stood on the site where W.H. Smith's now stands. Cleales, authorised Ford Dealers bought these premises when the Post Office moved from King Street to its present site in the High Street in 1919. And the Royal Coat of Arms can still be seen above the windows on the first floor. The amazing thing is, that such an imposing civic amenity should have enjoyed such a short reign!

In an article in the 'Saffron Walden Weekly News' dated Saturday, September 21st 1889, on 'The New Post Office Buildings' the writer says that 'rapid progress is being made on the new Post Office Buildings which will occupy a prominent position in King Street. The architects are Mr. F. J. Whiffin of Saffron Walden assisted by Messrs. Benison and Bargman (London).

He continues, 'the building is being built in the Renaissance style, red brick facings and Bath stone dressing being used for the purpose. The roof will be covered with Staffordshire tiles. The business accommodation will be most complete'.

It certainly was! The Postmaster's private apartments were on the first floor above the actual post-office itself, and above that, on the third floor were – the servants' bedrooms!

He then goes on to say that "a clock which will be of great service to the public will surmount the window.' Also, 'three shops are being built and utilised to the best advantage.' And 'persons wishing to secure prominent and well-adapted business premises will be fortunate in securing one of these.'

The Saffron Walden Post Office was inaugurated in 1635 as part of the countrywide Postal Service, the forerunner of the modern G.P.O. A brief outline of its history appears in the Official Brochure for the Charter 750 Celebrations, and reads as follows:-

'The local office appears to have been well patronised from the beginning, although by 1675, complaints about the inefficiency of deliveries in the town were commonplace. Ten years later, the office was considered of sufficient importance to the commercial life of Walden to pay a Deputy £45 per annum.'

In 1765, Saffron Walden was designated a postal town with its own postmark. The earliest known site of the Post Office was in the Butter Market, which stood in the Square before its demolition in 1845.

There is no record of a mail coach having a scheduled run to the town, but 'The Fly', the passenger service, appears to have coped with local needs. In 1845, the Post Office moved into the newly built Literary Institute and the room which now houses the children's library. Service was through a wicket, later replaced by a door, with the customers obliged to queue on the pavement. Mails at this time were delivered from Cambridge by cart, but 1850, their carriage became the sole right of the Eastern Railway Company.

It was at this time that Saffron Walden's deliveries were undertaken by a widow named Mercy Smith who would walk the streets wrapped in a heavy black cloak carrying her basket of letters. She was a woman of poor education frequently obliged to call on shop-keepers for the addresses to be read to her. She sorted the mails behind a shop, or else in the Corn Exchange, and not infrequently on a flat tombstone in the Churchyard.

King Street before Tarmacadam came along

In 1870, the telegraph was installed, and four years later the Post Office moved to the premises recently vacated by the Gibson Bank in Market Hill.

As local business began to prosper, so did the Post Office. In 1882, a sub-office was opened in Sewards End. The following year the main office began to issue postal orders and despatch parcels for the first time.

This increased trade brought the need for a further move, and in 1980, the Post Office moved to King Street.

It seems to us that Hardwicks the fishmongers has stood on the corner of King Street and Market Passage since time immemorial. And an interesting point is, that on the map of Walden for 1877 this is shown as the corner of what was then known as Fish Row.

Probably when Thomas Hardwick arrived at No. 9 King Street in 1872, it was merely an extension of a trade which had been carried on in this part of the town for centuries. For along what we know as Market Passage, the fishmongers of long ago would have set up their stalls to sell their wares.

The earliest records of Thomas Hardwick's business show it commenced at No. 12 Market Hill (next door to the Kings Arms) in 1800. In those early days he manufactured ginger beer, soda water, lemonade, pickles and sauces, as well as selling fish and fruit.

For well over a century, perhaps longer, the Butterfield family owned No. 9 King Street. Isaac Butterfield appears in the earliest rating lists of 1757, when No. 9 was described as 'house and chambers'. A hundred years later, George Butterfield (son or grandson?) was living there, described as 'Perfumer'.

But from 1872 until the late 1950s, generations of Hardwicks carried on a fishmongers' business on this site. And now, although it still remains essentially a fishmongers, only the name reminds us of the Hardwick family who, at the turn of the century, like all other Walden business people, lived over the shop.

Eva Scales, whose father had the Saddlery across the passage from Hardwicks, still remembers the thrill of going to parties at No. 9 when the highlight of the evening was the magic lantern show!

The Hardwicks, like so many old family businesses of yesterday, held their customers in great esteem. It was enough just to receive an order from them. Madam, or madam's housekeeper had no need to soil her hands by actually carrying the fish home herself. No – it would be delivered later in the day by the horse and cart, kept in Castle Street at the bottom of a small alleyway between Nos. 63A and 65.

There is a story of the wife of a prominent business man in the town, noted for her somewhat frugal ways.

Going into Hardwicks one day, she saw that herrings were being sold, seven for 6d – approx. 3p – and said to Mr. Hardwick, 'I will take seven herrings. You may deliver four today, and three tomorrow!'

Laughable as this story may seem, 80 years ago, tradesmen were only too pleased to deliver even the smallest item to their customers. A far cry from loading and unloading the supermarket trolley of today!

At some time in its long history, No. 9 was divided into two properties, the second part appearing in the records as No. 11.

Department of Environment notes state that No. 9 and 11 are all one 16th or early 17th century house, timber-framed and plastered. And the exposed timbers on the corner of Market Passage clearly show the tiny, original windows on the first floor.

Probably the property was divided at the time Thomas Hardwick bought No. 9. Because, from then onwards No. 11 appears to have been run as a tobacconist's shop. First by Alfred Rippon, later James Newman in 1896, and then Mrs. Augusta Green in 1930.

This is the shop which Bill Southern's father Sylvester Southern bought in 1938, the fore-runner of the highly successful confectionery and tobacconists of Lime Tree Passage.

Later, when Southerns moved down the street to No. 13 Gerald Pagano (now in Market Row) started his furnishing and lighting business here.

With the passing years however, No. 11 became once more part of the original No. 9 King Street, and that is how we know it today.

One of the most attractive features of No. 13 is the charming old-fashioned square-paned bay windows on either side of the doorway. Unfortunately, the right-hand window had been replaced by a plate-glass one at one stage. But when the Southerns took over, an aesthetically pleasing replica was made to match the other window on the left.

Records describe No. 13 as a small 17th century timber-framed and plastered house on an L-shaped plan with a gabled wing extending south at the rear (No. 5 Butchers Row). The north front (facing King Street) refaced in the early 19th century.

Rating lists of 1790 show that this was the premises of John Kent senior, the wellknown Saffron Walden clockmaker, whose son, John junior, set up his own business in the High Street next door to the Cross Keys.

The Kent family continued to live at No. 13 until 1856, when Sarah Kent (grand-daughter?) died. Sarah Kent was an ironmonger, and her assistant, Henry Wisby, inherited or bought the business after her death. In 1876, the property – which was copyhold to the Manor of Chipping Walden (Audley End Estate) passed into the hands of William Smith. Mrs. Eliza Smith (William's widow) and her four daughters lived at No. 13 from 1887 until 1914, using the two front rooms for business purposes.

In one Julia Smith had a hairdressing business, and in the other, her sister Kate ran an employment agency together with selling toys and cutlery.

At the rear of the shop in those days, there was, apparently, a tiny garden, hardly big enough for a cat to scratch in, but nevertheless, a treasured piece of earth!

It was in the early forties, Mr. S.A. Chilton opened his tobacconist's and confectionery shop at No. 13 and per-formed that philistine act of replacing one of the lovely 19th century windows with the modern plate-glass one.

When Southerns decided to enlarge their business and move further down King Street, Jennings, the Estate Agents took over No. 13.

No. 13 Jennnings the Estate Agents, now Talents Gift Shop

Mr. Ernest Jennings first came to Walden in 1906, buying an already established business from Mr. Slocombe at No. 5 Cross Street.

For 50 years Ernest Jennings, the Auctioneer and Estate Agent, was part of the established way of life in Saffron Walden. When he died in 1956, many farmers of the old-school, believed it was the end of an era.

Jennings moved to No. 13 in the late 70s, to become Sworder Jennings in more recent years, and Mr. Bruce Munro, partner in Sworders, is very much a local man and unashamed nostalgerian!

Bruce Munro was born in Thaxted and became an estate agent on the advice of his father, starting with Cheffins in Saffron Walden in May 1950.

'In those days,' he says, 'there were only two estate agents in the town – Cheffins and Jennings.'

One of Bruce Munro's first jobs was, to collect the rents from the many small cottages in streets like Castle Street, Bridge End, and Pleasant Valley.

'There were so many of them,' he says, 'primitive little places with outside lavatories, occupied by the same families for generation upon generation. The rents used to average between 3/6d (35p) and 7/6d (70p) a week. Now, these self-same cottages are very much in demand and they are snapped up as soon as they come on the market. Very few houses are available for renting these days.'

Mr. Munro talks about the early 50s as being the heyday of the great marquee sales, when the contents of some of the more imposing residences in Saffron Walden would be auctioned in a marquee on the lawn.

Most of the furniture would be handsome and valuable; largely 18th century antiques. He particularly remembers a fine Hepplewhite Bookcase belonging to the Adams, of Adams & Lang – the solicitors – which was sold for £400. 'Today,' he says, 'that bookcase would make £10,000 at an auction.'

In contrast, he reminisces about the monthly auctions in the Corn Exchange. In the early 50s furniture was rationed and many young couples relied on these sales to furnish their homes.

He says, 'we used to have as many as 500 lots, and it was all extremely entertaining. There was a large, rotund, Dickensian character, named Bill Mares, who had a shop at Sewards End. If no-one else wanted the stuff, it would be knocked down to Bill for 1/- (5p), and if he wouldn't take it, then Neville Cox would. Neville was a porter as well as a dealer, and he had a junk yard in Cross Street (now Martins the newsagents).

Mr. Munro continues, 'farm auctions took place at Michaelmas, after the harvest. Farms were much smaller in those days. Combine harvesters were just coming in, so there would be lots of farm machinery, thrashing drums, balers, binders, the odd horse or two, and the tractors would always be Fordson! The farmers were a canny lot, but then, farmers have always been canny!' Bruce Munro left Cheffins in 1960 to join Jennings. Across the road from Jennings, the gothic redevelopment of the late 19th century, now Godfreys, Stead & Simpson and Dewhursts, has obliterated for all time any trace of yet another Saffron Walden clockmaker.

Charles Pratt, whose grave can be found in the churchyard, had his house and shop on this site in the 1780's. He died at the age of 84, in 1829. William Archer, a Walden butcher, also had his premises on this site. Perhaps it was where Dewhursts now stands, but we shall never know, nor will we ever be certain that those 19th century planners were right to demolish the old to make way for the new.By the late 1970s 'The Hoops' public house in King Street had almost ceased to exist for many people. There were a few who remembered it from former years, when it played an important part in the life of the town. But for many, either it just wasn't there, or it had declined into a sad shadow of a previous age.

Since 1980 however, The Hoops has taken on a completely new lease of life. The ground floor has been given over to two modern shops, reflecting the trend of the late 20th century, and its upper storey has become a smart restaurant.

Records say The Hoops date back to the early 16th century – an old coaching Inn, refaced and altered in the early 19th century, when the roof was raised and an extension added to the east end.

Early photographs show it as an undistinguished-looking 19th century pub.

It was here that for many years the 'Saffron Bloom Lodge of Oddfellows' held their meeting in the large room (now the restaurant) on the first floor.

Local historian, Mr. Cliff Stacey, says, he recalls the awe-inspiring initiation ceremony when, as a juvenile member, he had to wait outside, until a spy-hole opened in the door, and a voice asked him for the password; after that he entered into a man's world – a member of the Adult Lodge of The Saffron Bloom Oddfellows!

Here also, the Buffaloes would meet, and even today, sometimes the restaurant is referred to as 'The Buffalo Room', with the old smoke vent in the ceiling. This was a necessary amenity when the Oddfellows and The Buffaloes would smoke, chat and drink their way through the evening.

There are those who believe The Hoops to be the original White Hart where Pepys stayed, but this has been proved untrue in recent years.

Possibly it could have been the Inn that gave King Street its name, again this is doubtful. The name – The Hoops – is referred to in a deed dating back to 1740. Further, recent evidence shows that, in medieval times it was probably a merchant's house with shops on the ground floor whose windows were open to the street – Cross Street.

Certainly by the 18th century it *was* an Inn. An extract from 'The Cambridge Chronicle' dated 1775, tells the following story:-

'Eleven Fenman from the Isle of Ely, being employed by Sir John Griffin Griffin in draining a part of his park at Audley End, went one evening to the Inn called The Hoops, to drink. After getting a little spirited they told the Maid they would give her sixpence each to fetch them as much beer as they could drink in single half-pints from the cellar. If they tired her she was to pay for the liquor. If she tired them, they were to pay for the whole.

The girl accepted the bet, although she had been washing all day; and drew them 517 single half-pints before they gave out, which were all drunk by the said men.

The distance from the room where they sat to the tap was measured; from which it appears she walked nearly twelve miles in fetching it; the quantity of liquor drank by each man was about three gallons in three hours. – The above is a fact'.

During the 1914 war, an arrow was painted on the Cross Street wall of The Hoops. It was one of a series of arrows throughout the town, all pointing in the same direction. The idea being that the whole population would evacuate in the same direction should the country be invaded.

But the end of the 70s saw the end of The Hoops as a public house. Thankfully it was bought by people whose affinity for old buildings allowed a gentle, rather than a rigorous, restoration, which in turn, has contributed greatly to the enhancement of King Street.

Bit by bit, the 19th century frontage was removed to reveal the original 16th century overhang. Medieval shop windows, plastered and painted over long years ago, were uncovered to disclose evidence of the shops which existed in Tudor times.

Hunt Brothers, one of the two shops now on the ground floor, is very much a shop of today. It specialises in luxury kitchens and domestic appliances.

Stephen and Veronica Hunt have been running their business at The Hoops for four years, as a continuation of an enterprise they started in the Central Arcade.

For Steve it was a natural extension of his career as a domestic appliance service engineer with the Westinghouse Company.

Next door is a completely different type of shop. Simply called 'Hoops'. Run by a quartet, who say that none of them have ever had any experience in shop-keeping before, it is now one of the most successful shops in Walden.

Specialising in clothes and arts and crafts, Hoops is a fascinating mixture of the unusual and the familiar. Ken and Gemma Rhodes live in Ashdon. For over 25 years, Ken, a lawyer, worked in London. Then, four years ago he bought half of The Hoops as an investment and he and Gemma were joined by Michael Yorke and her mother, Mary Dadd. Michael, known as 'Mickey' to her friends is the wife of Canon Michael Yorke, vice Provost of Chelmsford Cathedral, one-time rector of Ashdon.

Mary's husband, Christopher Dadd, was a director of The Royal Show at Stoneleigh, and Mary herself, responsible for the organisation of The Royal Pavilion.

Each member of the quartet brought their own highly individual ideas into the business, which is probably why Hoops is such a success.

If old buildings could speak, they would tell many strange tales, and in this respect Hoops is no exception. But it fell to Gemma Rhodes to tell me the story of the doll.

In one corner of the shop there stands a fine old corner cupboard with, quite rightly, a preservation order on it.

Unfortunately during the restoration of the premises, the young builders had scant regard for antiquity and knocked the cupboard down by mistake. Out from behind fell a little doll. A poor little thing, only 5" high, with a waxen face, a few shreds of hair and one leg.

Without a word, one of the workmen put the doll into his pocket. But that evening, as he rode home on his motor-bike, he had an accident, fell off, and hurt his leg badly.

'Here,' he said to his pal, who had stopped to help, 'take this doll back where it belongs.'

80

Shamefacedly the pal took the doll back to Hoops and handed it to another workman, who told the owners what had happened.

Mickey Yorke took the doll up to London to the Victoria and Albert Museum, who gave the opinion that the doll must be well over 300 years old.

Unanimously, it was decided amongst the quartet that the doll must go back where it belonged, behind the corner cupboard which had to be restored to its rightful place. 'And now, we like to think she brings us good luck,' says Gemma Rhodes with a smile.

Upstairs is a relaxing world of 1920s nostalgia. The Old Hoops Restaurant is the brain-child of 52 year-old Ken Kemp and his wife Wendy. Ken runs his own advertising agency in London, this is his first venture into being a restaurateur.

The decor of the restaurant is a reflection of Ken's personal taste and necessity. The room which once gave hospitality to the Oddfellows, the Buffaloes and the Shepherds, is large, cavernous and anonymous. It was also painted stark white when the Kemps took it over.

Now, dark green walls with glass-shaded lamps; old French bentwood chairs, and hanging baskets spilling with real plants (nothing, absolutely nothing plastic) complements Ken's collection of old advertising memorabilia.

Continuing on our way down the street we come to No. 17, known as 'Dobsons', which, together with Nos. 19 and 21 are all one late 15th century Hall House.

They are best appreciated from the opposite side of the road, where the jettied gables, each with its original bargeboards, carved with winged dragons may be clearly seen. And although altered during the 18th and 19th centuries, many of the original features have been retained or exposed during recent decades.

But No. 17 displays most of the important features of this building – exposed timber framing, heavy angle bracket and shaft with moulded capitals and base. The shop front facing King Street is however, 20th century, with a doorway made from a medieval window.

Facing Cross Street there are two original windows with trefoil heads, on the first storey, and four medieval shop windows and a door (now used as a window) similar to its near neighbour The Hoops.

Again, like The Hoops, these windows would be open to the street, and protected by wooden shutters at night and during bad weather. Which is all evidence that this was an important part of the town from the point of view of trade.

Old rating lists dating from 1794 show that the whole property – Nos. 17 to 21 – belonged to John Randall. John Randall must have died in 1804, and consequently the house was split into three units. So we may assume that, in view of the medieval windows and the size and construction of the building, like The Hoops, it probably belonged to a wealthy merchant who displayed his wares on the ground floor.

From 1820 to 1826 a carpenter named John Searle lived and worked at No.17, presumably using the shops as his work-shop. Later, in 1826, John Porter took over the premises which, according to records were 'improved'.

In 1828 James Wedd, a sadler came to No.17 to be succeeded later by his son Peter, in 1886. He stayed there until 1906, when Mr. T. Scales, also a saddler, arrived there with his family. His daughter Eva, still lives in Walden, but tells me she can remember very little of the actual building.

She does however, remember Miss Petch, who lived in Radwinter Road with her widowed mother, and rented one of the two front rooms where she taught music and typewriting.

The Scales did not stay long at No.17 and eventually Mr. Dobson, the barber from across the road at No.4 King Street – later to become The Librarian's House – moved into the premises.

Mr. Dobson seems to have died soon afterwards and Mrs. Dobson, a widow with two children, carried on the business, engaging a Mr. Bassett to do the barbering in the rear of the shop, whilst she ran a tobacconists in the front.

So Dobsons became what it has remained for many years, a tobacconists and sweet shop, until Mrs. Joy Dean and her partner, Mr. John Essex took Dobsons over fourteen months ago. Now the front part of the shop is still given over to sweets and tobacco, but the rear shop sells high quality leather goods.

Mrs. Dean and Mr. Essex have been selling leather goods for over 25 years and came to Walden from Bridge Street, Cambridge.

They say they find it extremely amusing when people who have lived away from the town for 40 or 50 years, return and expect to find the shop exactly as it was when they left. 'They even expect to find the same things on the shelves in exactly the same position as they used to be,' laughs Mr. Essex.

No.21 comprises the west gable end of the Hall House, and has, for many years been established as an opticians. First by Mr. Arthur Gatward, later by Mr. S.J. Williams. But this was the first shop that young Henry Hart bought in 1836. When he moved in 1886, William Steven opened his florists and seedsman's business and it was here that he had his warehouse and stables.

Steven was succeeded by Robert Petch at the turn of the century and then C.T. Watson who had his nurseries in Radwinter Road.

But for many people No.21 will always be remembered as the Co-op Confectionery in the 1930s.

Across the road Nos. 18 and 20, now Olivers Shoe Shop and Peter Dominic's wine merchants, are part of what was once described as a 'Genteel Family Residence'.

Actually, there is very little left of what must have been a very imposing, and architecturally pleasing building, described by D. of E. notes as, 'a 17th century house with red brick front, said to have been built in 1633.' All that remains now however, is a lovely old roof and charming upper storey windows.

These were the premises bought by Henry Hart (see page 84). He bought them at an auction at the Rose & Crown Hotel on Saturday 19th May 1866, at sometime between four and five o'clock in the afternoon.

The house was described as having a 'commanding frontage, replete with every convenience, a paved yard, large ornamental walled garden, also a messuage used as a printing office.' This latter was the two cottages which Henry rented for his printing works.

Details in the fine print at the bottom of the auction notice might give a clue as to how King Street got its name. 'The

Auctioneer begs to call particular attention of Professional and Commercial Gentlemen to this highly important offer of Property, it being situate in the best business part of the town, and has for many years past been the site of an *extensive Family Brewing Trade.'*

Moreover, if we walk a little further down King Street, to where the road narrows, we will come to a 16th century archway. This led to Henry Hart's yard and garden.

The archway and the pavement beneath still belong to Mr. Jack Turnbull (Edwin's son) and Mr. Turnbull says that the archway is the remains of an old Coaching Inn – probably one of the earliest Inns in the town. This I believe may have been the original King's Arms.

The archway links Nos.22 and 26 described by the D. of E. as 'a late 15th century house built on a half-H shaped plan with wings extending north on either side of a wagon-way, which still remains. The house was extensively altered in the late 18th and 19th centuries, and is now 2 tenements of different periods...The original wagon-way between Nos.22 and 26 has chamfered oak jams, a moulded 4-centered head with foliated spandrals, exposed timber framing with heavily moulded beams and joists and narrowly spaced studs. There are the remains of other carved details...'

Walk through the archway and look upwards and you will see a doorway. Probably stage coaches were drawn through the archway, and the passengers travelling on top of the coach with the luggage, would have entered the Inn by climbing a ladder lowered from this doorway.

In 1930 the cottages which had been Henry Hart's original printing works were destroyed by fire. At the same time a Brewhouse or Inn, called the Tailor's Arms, (now Chew & Osborne's) was also destroyed.

It is an interesting fact that Henry Hart bought the property from William Burrows who, in the 1851 census list is described as a 'Brewer'.

Going back through the old rating lists, we also find that in 1790, James Searle, the Banker, owned these premises. As we have already learned, the Searles set up in opposition to the Gibsons as Maltsers at a later date. Whether the fact that the property contained a Brewhouse and was probably all part of the old Coaching Inn, influenced the Searles in anyway, we shall never know.

Newdales, Baxters and Glasswells are three shops standing on a site that was known in King Street for many years as 'Robsons'.

Robsons had originally been founded in 1760 by Thomas Day and his wife, Susanna (nee Crafton) as a grocers, corn-chandlers, drapers and general stores, and must have been where Newdales is now.

Thomas and Susanna were Quakers, and like all good Quakers in Walden in those days, their business prospered, probably because Susanna herself was a remarkably clever woman in her own right.

She was a talented silhouettist, and writer. Her journal 'A memoranda for the Help of Recollection' kept from 1797 to 1804 is still retained in its little leather binding in the Friends House, and is a valuable record of a middle-aged Quaker during the Napoleonic Wars.

Susanna helped run her husband's business, and at the same time care for her four children and the apprentices. One of these apprentices, Joseph Marks Green married the Days' daughter and the shop became known as Day & Green.

Later, another marriage to another apprentice, brought in the name Robson, and by 1850, the business became known as 'Robson & Company.'

Robson & Company flourished. By 1886 'Robson & Sons' owned Nos.23 to 27 and were recorded in the town almanack for that year as 'Cabinet Makers, Drapers and Grocers.' By the late 1880s they had taken over Richard Bevington Shewell's Drapery establishment across the road (next door to the archway).

But with the turn of a new century, the fortunes of Robsons appeared to decline. By 1911 Robsons were no longer on the North side of King Street.

In 1936, No. 23 (Thomas Day's first shop) was acquired by Sidney Valentine, who ran the business until the late 60s under the name ' Walter Robson.'

From the outside at least, this always appeared a sad little shop, but the assistants were always extremely helpful and courteous. And it was one of those useful little shops, beloved by the home-dressmaker, now so hard to find in these days of pre-packaging.

Now bicycles and motor car accessories have taken the place of the rolls of dress material which seemed to forever grace the windows. And on which, at Christmas time, there would be added a small white label with the words 'Xmas Gift'.

Perhaps Glasswells, the furnishers is a continuation of Robsons. Founded in Bury St. Edmunds by Mr. Gerry Glasswell, in Brentdovel Street, in 1946, they came to Saffron Walden in 1951.

It was Mr. Gerry's idea to give pensioners a small gift of tea and sugar at Christmas time. A custom that was started the very first Christmas, and which has continued, and will continue for as long as Glasswells continues, says his nephew, Mr. Terry Glasswell.

The decision to open-up in Saffron Walden was because of the town itself. 'It was a market town,' says Terry Glasswell. 'Just the sort of town we like to serve. Further, we believe in operating in a fairly local area so that our customers can benefit from a more personalised service, and Saffron Walden is very much in our area.'

Sadly, Mr. Gerry Glasswell died in 1981 at the age of 87.

No doubt there are many people in the town who remember Glasswells as the old 'Food Office' during the second world war. Just as they must remember the Home & Colonial Stores a little further down, where Mr. Archie Lansdowne used to be manager.

It is difficult to allocate exact numbers to certain properties. A study of old town almanacks will show that numbers altered time and time again when property was rebuilt, altered and amalgamated with adjoining buildings.

On the north side of the street, Nos 28 to 32, according to records, were formerly known as 24, 24A and 26 and are in fact, a 17th century timber-framed and plastered building with an 18th century brick front.

No.28, now Jodie Leather, was once the premises of Mr. Francis Furlong the Gunsmith. It was here that John Furlong, Gunmaker, set up his shop on this site in 1851, to be continued by his son until 1934.

Mr. Russell Walkyier of The Gunshop in the High Street, says that there are still a number of Furlong guns very much in use in the area. And certainly 'old Mr. Furlong' (Francis) is still remembered by a good many people in the town.

Nuts in May, at No.32, is a tiny shop, nearly always crowded. It combines a delightfully friendly atmosphere with an old-fashioned courtesy which makes it a typical Saffron Walden shop, despite the fact that it has only been in existence for about seven years.

Why Nuts in May? 'It just came out of the air,' says proprietor Tony Gill. 'We wanted an original, slightly humorous name which would stick in the minds of the public, and suddenly one day – there it was!' Undoubtedly a good name! The Gills must stock just about every variety of nut there is, as well as all the various pulses and cereals that go to make up a Whole-food diet.

Tony and his wife Peggy became interested in Wholefoods when living in Wiltshire. At a party, the highlight of the evening was a film show by 'Friends of the Earth', and the discussion which followed sowed the seeds of a new train of thought for the Gills. What started out as a casual interest, with experiments with different types of Wholefood, was to become a new way of life for them. Tony and Peggy had lived in the Saffron Walden area before moving to Wiltshire, and always kept up their old friendships, so, when the opportunity to buy No.32 arose, they jumped at the idea of turning their hobby into a business and moving back to the town.

Next door to the Cross Keys is a small cottage-type shop, now Moore's fashions, but for a long time known to the older generation in Walden as 'Wabons'- a sweet shop and fruiterers.

The last shop on the south-side of King Street is Bacon's, an old-established business of fruit and fish retailers. Now the shop is given over entirely to fruit and vegetables, and the proprietor, Mr. Frank Bacon, represents the fourth generation of this old family concern.

It all started when the railways came to Saffron Walden. This meant that fresh fish could be brought straight from the coast to the town everyday, and Frank Bacon's great-grandfather literally took the opportunity in both hands, pushing a fish barrow round the streets of a town very different from the Saffron Walden of today.

His son, William, built a house and shop in Station Street in 1911 (now Saffhire) – the first two properties to be built in that street – and began to smoke his own fish.

Eventually William's son took over the Station Street business, whilst *his* son, Frank, opened a shop in the High Street in 1960 (now the Job Centre). Later, Frank opened a second shop – No.43 King Street.

Many people will remember No.43 before the first World War, when it was Hiltons' Shoe Shop, and the manager was a young man named Walter DeBarr, founder of yet another well known, old-established family business in Walden.

EXCLUSIF

ASK ANYONE WHO HAS A MIELE KITCHEN.

If you have a friend who is fortunate enough to own a Miele kitchen, ask her about Miele quality and finish.

Ask her about all the practical details that only time and experience can prove.

Ask her about the amazing range of designs and finishes she had to select from.

If she lives in the area, she's probably a customer of ours: so ask her about our total service, which starts with planning, covers the complete installation and never really ends as long as you want a friendly helping hand.

Then you might be half-way prepared for the wide range of superb Miele kitchens and sound advice you will find when you call in at our showroom.

HUNT BROS.
(DOMESTIC APPLIANCES) LTD.
13a King Street,
Saffron Walden, Essex.
Tel. 0799-23088.

Miele

HARTS

the

CHARTER BOOKSELLERS

EST. 1836

Have been selling books in
Saffron Walden for over

150 Years!

ATLASES, MAPS:ORDNANCE SURVEY
MICHELIN GUIDE BOOKS
BOOKS OF LOCAL INTEREST
BARGAIN BOOKS

*Books not in stock can
be especially ordered!*

HARTS BOOKSHOP

5 KING STREET, SAFFRON WALDEN,
TEL(0799)23456.

GAYHOMES

Established 1965

Quality Housewares & Gifts

Market Place Saffron Walden Tel (0799) 23535

Eaden Lilley

Market Place Saffron Walden 26650

Elegant Fashion Collections
perfectly complemented by
Stylish Accessories . . .
Skincare, Make-up & Fragrance
by Lancôme and Esteé Lauder . . .
French Perfumes . . .

crowned by
"Rooftops"
– a delightful Restaurant.

Shopping in Saffron Walden has
never been so fashionable!

90

CHAPTER FOUR

AUDLEY ROAD

First published in the Saffron Walden Weekly News
August 23 – 30, 1984

The latter half of the 20th century finally eliminated what had once been little more than a country lane leading from "Cuckstoolende" (High Street south) to "Suardsende" (Sewards End), turning it into the urban thoroughfare we know as Audley Road.

Even as late as 1894, Audley Road was still largely undeveloped. True, earlier in the century fine mansions built by wealthy men of the town began to impose themselves upon this country lane.

In 1600 an orchard graced the corner where the Baptist Chapel now stands, and beyond that a "pightle" – parcel of land enclosed by a hedge – probably used for grazing – was to remain until the beginning of the 19th century.

But by 1750, the name "Highwaie from Cuckstoolende to Suardsende" was to become "Bailey's Lane" named after the farm on the site where Ingleside Court now stands. And by 1873 the appellation Audley Road gave prestige to the lane which now contained the houses of the rich and influential.

Perhaps the arrival of the Baptist Chapel in 1774 finally sealed the fate of Bailey's Lane.

The Manse belonging to the Chapel – No.55 Audley Road – is a distinguished, early 19th century building.

It was built in 1813 by the Chapel Trustees to provide a home for the young minister – 27 year-old Josiah Wilkinson and his bride, Elizabeth Leaper.

Later, at sometime in the 1870s, additional accommodation was added to house the growing family of the Rev. Alfred Rollason.

91

If we cross the road, we get a good sideways view of the original Baptist Chapel which was superseded by the 19th century Chapel built on to the western end. This former, more elegant building, was then relegated in 1879 to play the role of schoolhouse, pastor's study and library.

Walking past the Chapel and Manse, we catch a glimpse of Oasthouse Court – a complex of modern houses on the site of yet another old maltings, which originally belong to Jabez Gibson.

We now come to No.51 – Audley Cottage – an interesting brick and flint house, its highly ornamental bargeboards telling of an age when money was plentiful and labour cheap.

Audley Cottage was built by John Segar Wilkinson in 1857 for his bride Kate Evangeline Du Pont, whose great-niece Margaret, lives not a stone's throw away in nearby Tanner's Way.

Next door to Audley Cottage once stood the fine old mansion – Elm Grove – built by Jabez Gibson in 1828, whose grounds extended as far as his house in Hill Street (now the Municipal Offices) and with the typical feature of most Gibson properties – a tunnel in the garden – connecting both houses.

One entrance to the tunnel can still be seen in Jubilee Gardens, a small archway decorated inside with relief mouldings, but the tunnel itself was filled in many years ago.

Although Jabez Gibson owned Elm Grove, he does not appear to have actually lived in the house himself. Earliest records show that it was occupied by George Youngman from about 1839 to 1863, and Youngman's widow until 1878. After that it belonged to Jabez's youngest son, Edmund Birch Gibson, who entered the family banking business.

It was Edmund who removed some of the clothfold panelling from Hill House (quite legitimately) and installed it in the hall of Elm Grove.

A man of many interests, including milling and farming, he owned most of Little Walden, and was twice Mayor of Walden. And as we have learned before, it was he who planted the plane trees in the High Street in 1902 to mark the Coronation of Edward VII.

Elm Grove was bought during the very late 1960s as part of a project to provide sheltered accommodation for the elderly

An idea envisaged by Sir Foster Sutton, Dr. Gladys Gray and others.

Unfortunately, converting the actual house itself proved too costly, and therefore it was decided to demolish it and build small, self-contained bungalows on the site. Even this solution proved to be beyond the limits of available funds and after an application for a local authority grant had been turned down, the whole scheme was taken over by the Hanover Housing Trust.

Although there are few traces of the old mansion now, thankfully the superb wrought-iron gates remain. Wonderful examples of the blacksmith's art, they must have been made locally – probably by John Green whose iron foundry was in nearby West Road.

Elm Grove now consists of a group of small bungalows, each with its own tiny garden, where elderly people may enjoy complete independence, secure in the knowledge that there is always somebody close at hand should they need help.

Staff and residents at Elm Grove

That "somebody" is Mrs. Margery Overton. Mrs. Overton has been Warden of Elm Grove since it first opened nine years ago. She says she dearly loves her job, and feels that both she and her husband are part of one large family.

Margery Overton however, came as no stranger to Elm Grove. She remembers it from the days of her childhood, when it belonged to a wealthy bachelor named Mr. Brown.

"Mr. Brown" was Alderman Herbert Brown J.P., a prominent member of the Baptist Chapel, who often opened his house and grounds to the people of the Chapel for special functions.

He was especially fond of little children, and every year the Baptist Sunday School Treat would be held in the grounds of Elm Grove. It was he who provided all the prizes and sweets for the Treat, and escorted the children round his garden and greenhouses, pointing out all the exotic plants growing there.

One of these children was Mrs. Overton, and another Mr. Donald Purkiss the local architect.

Mr. Purkiss says, 'as a special treat he would take us to his Hothouse, where he had a plant that – if you were especially good – he would let you touch one of the leaves which would immediately shrivel up. I think it was some kind of tropical fern.'

He goes on to say, 'he would often ask some of us local tots to a party, and we used to sit round and have tea. When we had finished the meal, he used to have some of us sit on his knee. Then he would get out his old hunter watch and get it to chime.

'After that, he would give us all comics, and we would all go into his smoking room . He would put on his smoking jacket, get his pipe out, and we would sit round reading comics whilst he smoked.

'Sometimes we wanted to go to the toilet, and I remember this was lit by a skylight, and had hydrangeas growing in it.

'There was also a white cockatoo which lived in the summerhouse.'

Two of the main features of Elm Grove in its heyday were the folly and the summerhouse.

The folly – built of brick and flint, looking like a miniature church with a round, castellated tower – housed a small

The Folly at Elm Grove

museum. Unfortunately, this charming feature was almost completely destroyed when an enormous beech tree fell on top of it during a storm a few years ago.

Now, unless something is done to at least partially restore the folly and render it safe, it will disappear forever.

More substantial, but still requiring a little attention, is the summerhouse with its "Hangman's Stone.'

The Hangman's Stone with its curious hole like an unblinking eye, carries its own legend.

For a long time it stood in a field near to the Village of Littlebury. And Lord Braybrooke, who owned the land, gave Jabez Gibson permission to remove it to the garden of Elm Grove.

According to records, similar stones are to be found in at least six different parts of Britain, all carrying the same legend.

"A sheep stealer stole a sheep one night; tied its legs together and passed the rope over his head, and proceeded to carry it home on his back.

But the sheep was heavy and, seeing a stone of convenient height, the man paused to lean against it. Unfortunately, the animal struggled and kicked, and eventually slipped over the other side of the stone, thereby strangling the man. Next morning man and beast were discovered each hanging from opposite sides of the stone.

An indentation runs across the top of the stone and is believed to have been made by the friction of the rope caused by the struggles of the man and the animal."

Probably the real truth will never be known about the origins of this large boulder, but nevertheless, the legend makes a good tale.

For many people however, Elm Grove means Junior House School, with its headmistress Jeanne Barrie, for that is the last important role the old house played before it was finally pulled down.

Opposite Elm Grove stands Elm Grove Lodge, believed to have been the coachman's cottage, and connected in the old days to the big house by means of a primitive form of telephone – probably a speaking tube.

Elm Grove Lodge is a late 19th century building, many gabled, with elaborate bargeboards and woodwork, and a battery of massive chimneys. It is undeniably a superb example of Victorian Gothic carried to extremes, but the end result is an enchanting, fairytale cottage which might have slipped from the pages of a children's book.

Reed Lodge – a charming "thatched cottage" a few yards further down Audley Road, also belonged to the Elm Grove estate. But Reed Lodge, far from being a humble home, was almost an estate in itself, with grounds extending as far as Fairycroft, South Road, Station Road and probably Debden Road.

It is now the home of Mr. and Mrs. Raymond Hobbs. Mr. Hobbs – one time Managing Director of Saffron Walden Engineering Company – is now a semi-retired consulting and manufacturing engineer. He and his wife Muriel and their family have lived at Reed Lodge for over thirty years.

Reed Lodge was originally a small cottage or farmhouse belonging to one of the many farms in the neighbourhood during the 17th century.

Mr. Hobbs possesses deeds going back to 1799, but thinks that, judging from some of the massive timbers found in the cottage, it could probably date back to the 15th century.

When Jabez Gibson bought the land and cottage, he clad the timber-framed building with Suffolk bricks, and either he or his son at a later date, added two wings of Cambridgeshire bricks.

Now a rich man's house with stone mullioned windows and high ceilinged, well-proportioned rooms, the original cottage forms the central portion of the house.

At one period in its history, Edmund Birch Gibson is believed to have lived here after buying it from his son-in-law, Arthur Midgeley – only to return it at a later date.

Typical again of a Gibson property – Reed Lodge possesses an underground tunnel system, fed by air from one of the three enormous chimneys which serves as a ventilating shaft for tunnels leading to both Elm Grove and Fairycroft.

In 1892 Mr. Charles Stewart Douglas Wade the local solicitor, and his wife, Esme, moved into Reed Lodge which at that time was known as "Reed Cottage."

It was here that his son – Emlyn Capel Stewart – was born in 1894 – later to become a distinguished lawyer and Downing Professor of English Law. However, shortly before the arrival of their second son – now Major-General (Douglas) Ashton (Lofft) Wade, in 1898 – they moved to The Grove (Eastacre) or Chater's Hill.

But the property, having belonged to various members of the Gibson family over the years, was eventually sold in 1923 after the death of Alexander Gibson.

After a succession of owners, Mr. Hobbs' father bought the house as a speculative venture, but Raymond Hobbs, who had already started to build a half-timbered house for his growing family, begged his father to sell it to him.

'It was the sort of house I had always wanted,' says Raymond Hobbs with a smile, 'and since we moved in during the 1950s we have always been very happy here. Over the years I have made some modifications, but always bearing in mind the age and type of property I was dealing with.'

It was Mr. Hobbs who told me the amusing story of the storks belonging to Elm Grove.

During the short time his father owned Reed Lodge, a maiden lady of impeccable character owned Elm Grove. And at that time two fine storks made of cast iron adorned the brick plinths at each end of the flint wall fronting the mansion. Mr. Hobbs' father could not resist teasing the lady, warning her of the sort of things storks were wont to bring.

Imagine everyone's surprise when, one night, the storks mysteriously disappeared, never to be seen again. Their removal was never commented upon by their owner, and Mr. Hobbs was allowed to think whatever he chose.

After many years of searching, Raymond Hobbs finally managed to trace one of the missing storks, albeit broken, but not beyond repair. This, he intends to mend at some early date and, rather than tempt providence again, place it on his own wall, facing its former home.

Next door to Reed Lodge stands another large house – Falcon Grove.

Falcon Grove was built by Charles Erswell in 1850 on land which was part of a bequest by Edmund Birch Gibson to a Mr. Jones – who presumably sold it to Charles Erswell.

Charles Erswell lived at Falcon Grove for a few years then, in 1856, sold the house to Joshua Clarke.

I have been told that Joshua Clarke never actually lived there himself. In 1862 however, he rented the property to Joseph Robson, the prominent Saffron Walden businessman, who appears to have lived there until 1891.

Who occupied Falcon Grove next is not quite clear but, in 1914, Joshua Clarke's widow sold the house to another Saffron Walden businessman – Gray Palmer, the Outfitter.

Gray Palmer's widow, Clara, sold the house in 1921 to Mr. D.H.B. Jones who, in turn, sold it to Councillor Leslie Godfrey in 1927.

This one time Mayor of the Town took a very active interest in the life of Walden, and rendered many valuable services to the Community, especially in connection with the Almshouses, Hospital and the Literary Institute.

In 1974 however, the house was sold yet again, this time to Eric Paice the wellknown Television playwright. Nine years later it again changed hands when Mr. Stephen Rapkin and his wife Vickie bought it.

Falcon Grove itself is a delightful example of early Victorian architecture. And Vickie Rapkin has been careful to choose her furnishings to complement and enhance the fine, well-proportioned rooms.

A Victorian Folly in the garden in the form of a tall, brick and flint tower, and a splendid old coach house – now a double garage with studio above, reminds us that, Falcon Grove – like its close neighbours – was built by a rich man!

Returning once more to the opposite side of the road we come to Fairycroft House, another Audley Road mansion. It was built by Charles Fiske, between 1830 and 1831 and named after the large pasture on which it stands.

Charles Fiske was one of three brothers, all surgeons – believed by some to be the first surgeons in Saffron Walden. He died in 1844 leaving his widow to live on at Fairycroft House until 1849 when Joshua Clarke the maltster bought it.

Fairycroft, now a crumbling ghost-like shadow of its former self is a typical Regency Mansion, with what was once

Fairycroft House

99

a spacious, well cultivated garden – now alas, just a collection of rotting huts and a car park.

It is the home of the local Youth Community Centre, but will be remembered by many as the A.R.P. Headquarters during the Second World War.

In the grounds of the old mansion stands a hut – this, a silent comment on priorities set by local and national government, is the Department of Social Services.

Forty-eight year-old Mr. John Pettit is Area Organiser for Social Services for Uttlesford District. A position he has held for the last four years.

Mr. Pettit's duties include the administration of care for the elderly; mentally ill and handicapped and the physically handicapped; also the numerous residential and day-care establishments, including the Home Help Services.

With a staff of over 40, including 27 social workers of varying grades, plus a large number of staff located at various centres, Mr.Pettit is quick to stress the importance of the many volunteers in the area, without whose help the work of the Social Services would be impossible.

Continuing our walk, we come to No.29, the end house in a terrace of four solid, red-brick Victorian villas. These pleasant, time-enduring old houses are a compromise between Victorian Gothic and Essex Hall house. Built in 1879, they represent a continuation of the gentle mellowness so characteristic of Audley Road.

No.29 has been the home of Mrs. Joyce MacElroy for 30 years. Previously the house belonged to – the Miss Bells – formidable ladies who "wrote"!

Miss Mary was a poet, and published her own slim volume in 1931, entitled "Tree Blossom" – a copy can be seen in the Town Library.

Miss Lucy had two books to her credit – "The Art of Public Speaking" and "The Public Speakers' Dictionary" – a subject which she taught for many years – copies of these are also in the Town Library.

Mrs. MacElroy also writes poetry – 'but just for my own amusement,' she says.

Nevertheless, she did start a highly successful poetry group in Saffron Walden which continued for ten years, and volumes of poetry, written by local poets are still to be found in the Town Library.

Once again we cross the road, this time to visit No.24.

This is the house where ex-Mayor Russell Green was born, and this is the house where he still lives with his wife Marion and their three daughters, Rachel (20), Emma (18) and Mary (15).

It is a solid, red-brick, turn-of-the century family house bought by Mary Green, Russell's grandmother for her son James.

James, a foreman engine driver on the railway was Mary's only son who, for some years had been living and working in

Mary Downham Green in her old age

Cambridge. But when he married for a second time, Mary now a widow, begged James to return to his native Walden. And as an inducement, promised to buy him a house.

It was Florence, James' second wife who chose No.24 Audley Road. And Mary, true to her word, went to look at it with her cousin Elizabeth Day. And, having approved of what she saw, paid the asking price – £300 – a substantial sum in the 1920s – in cash, on the spot, all in gold sovereigns'!

Mary, James' eldest daughter had been instrumental in bringing her father and Florence together.

Mary, who worked at Chivers Jam Factory in Sawston, became friendly with Florence Mason, a young widow whose husband had been killed in the First World War. And at Christmas time that year, Mary confided in her new friend that her mother had recently died in childbirth, and she, Mary, would have to cook Christmas dinner for her father and ten brothers and sisters, and didn't know how she was going to cope. And, taking advantage of their friendship, she begged Florence to come and cook Christmas Dinner for them.

Cooking Christmas Dinner for James Green and his family and her own baby daughter was the prelude to what was to become a regular weekly arrangement. Until eventually, James – although quite a bit older than Florence – asked her to marry him and was accepted.

So Florence and James set up home at No.24 and Florence bore James ten more children – Russell being the baby of the family – his father's 21st child!

After leaving the Boys' British School at the age of 15, Russell was all set to train as a dental mechanic for the local dental surgeon, Mr. Fish. But – by this time his father was dead and his mother had taken a lodger – Mr. Herbert Peasgood, Builder and Carpenter of Gold Street.

Mr. Peasgood thought young Russell – who had good marks at school for carpentry – had great potential as a carpenter and joiner. So Florence took out an indenture of apprenticeship with Mr. Peasgood on behalf of her youngest son.

Russell was not entirely happy with the situation He explains, 'it was a small place in a small town, and when you are young you look a little bit further than a small place in a small town.'

Besides, the glamour of the footlights had been beckoning Russell for a good many years. Ever since that, as a small child in the Second World War, he had entertained the troops stationed nearby with his tap-dancing.

He had also been "discovered" by Maisie Lynn – a dancer with her own Troup. Performing in Walden she had witnessed Russell's talent as a tap-dancer and asked his mother if she could take him back to London to train as a professional. But Florence was not anxious to relinquish her youngest child.

It was at this time also, that Russell had become an object of ridicule at school – all because he enjoyed tap-dancing! But a far-sighted and understanding teacher – Joyce Trinder – persuaded Russell to take up amateur theatricals instead.

Miss Trinder taught drama at the Youth Centre. And, it was as a member of her drama group, competing in a local drama festival, that Russell Green won an award for being the best amateur actor of the year.

It was the beginning of a long career in amateur theatricals for Russell. A career which has brought him into contact with many famous people, including Brian Rix and Richard Baker.

However, despite his success on the local Boards, Russell yearned to see the world beyond Saffron Walden, and thought his big chance had come when he had to report for National Service.

Unfortunately he was turned down because of a punctured ear-drum. So it was back to Gold Street and Peasgoods, whose building trade was rapidly developing into an Undertaking business as well

Russell says he remembers quite vividly the first time he was asked to be a coffin bearer. When he got inside the church he fainted right away! The kindly Vicar thought it was the emotional strain which had overcome the young man.

'In fact, 'says Russell, 'it was because I'd been to a party the night before and was feeling the effect of it! You see,' he explained, 'I actually drink very little alcohol – I must be allergic to it or something – because it always makes me very ill indeed – even if I have only a small amount!'

At the age of 30 Russell married the girl next door. Only at that particular time, Marion wasn't actually living next door!

As secretary to the manager of Barclays Bank, Marion, who comes from Haverhill, came to live next door to the Greens as a lodger. And although she had been warned of Russell's roving eye by her landlady, she quite enjoyed his teasing whenever they met.

Even after she moved into a flat of her own, they still remained friends. It was when Russell was in hospital recovering from an operation on his tonsils and Marion was visiting him, prior to going off on holiday, that things came to a head.

'You don't think much of me if your are going away on holiday and leaving me in hospital,' he said reproachfully.

'Is that a proposal of marriage then?' asked Marion somewhat taken aback.

'We got engaged on Christmas Eve,' says Russell. 'It was at midnight communion at St. Mary's and I slipped the ring on her finger when the Vicar said – do this in remembrance of me. And I heard a woman behind us whisper to her companion – they're getting engaged!'

When asked about his activities in local politics Russell admits that in the beginning he wasn't the slightest bit interested, knowing nothing about them at all. But Labour Councillor Peter Preece, a prospective candidate for the then Borough Council, suggested Russell should also stand. And his mother – always a staunch Labour woman – finally persuaded him.

'So, I stood for Council and got in,' he says, 'and I have been on the Council ever since.

'Once you become a local Councillor,' he continues, 'you soon learn that people have problems, and it is up to you to help them solve their problems.

'But,' he emphasises, 'I never think of any problem in a political light. And this is how I became involved with the St. Raphael Club and the Mentally Handicapped – because the problem there was – they could not get anyone to entertain them!'

The Almanack for 1939 tells us that No.19 Audley Road was – The Priory School, Principal Miss M.P. Cunningham. Was this also the location of the earlier Trinity College? The Principal, Mr. Samuel Benstead, was, according to a testimonial from the Rev. W. Scott M.A., "a young man of considerable attainments, great industry and perseverance, and gifted with ability of an uncommon degree."

Mr. Benstead ran a boarding school between the years 1886–1896, which I can only assume must have been the same building which houses the Priory School at a later date.

Despite all his many attributes, poor Mr. Samuel Benstead does not appear to have made much of an academic impression on Saffron Walden and, after 1897, he disappears without a trace.

As we walk towards the end of the road – which is really the beginning – the houses, especially on the south side, take on a twentieth century air. This is because for many years, the land consisted of nurseries and pasture. It was the last bit of Audley Road to become urbanised – but that is a story for another day.

Let us look at No.1 Audley Road. Again a tall, solid, red-brick turn-of-the-century house; the home of the late Dr. Gordon Jacob, C.B.E.

Dr. Jacob died earlier this year, shortly before his 89th birthday. Before his retirement in 1966 he was Professor of Theory, Composition and Orchestration at the Royal College of Music.

Educated at Dulwich College and the Royal College of Music, he studied orchestration under the late Vaughan Williams.

He was considered one of the greatest authorities on orchestration, and his book "Orchestral Technique – a manual for Students" is acclaimed to be the best students' text-book of its kind.

Although he composed many piano, violin and oboe concertos and other orchestral works – including a symphony, chamber music and part songs – he also composed music for the Radio Show "Itma" during the grim days of the Second World War, and was for many years connected with the light music programme of the B.B.C.

Now let us cross the road once again and look at the large house on the corner of a comparatively new housing estate called Farmadine.

Samuel Fiske, brother of Charles, built Farmadine in 1821 – according to the inscription on the brick and flint wall.

He died in 1856. Like his brother, who built Fairycroft, he was a surgeon, and like his father before him, he was a Mayor of Saffron Walden.

Undoubtedly Farmadine was once a splendid country mansion with extensive grounds reaching as far as Station Road and probably beyond.

Today the old house has been turned into flats and possesses little of its former glory. Slightly crumbling in parts, its brick and flint stable block housing a builder's office, it stands, a mere token of a way of living that has gone forever, to be mourned by some and applauded by others. The once-lovely garden and trees destroyed to make way for a different kind of life.

Lay's

TEA AND COFFEE SPECIALISTS

Over 80 different varieties from which to choose.

We also carry a large range of coffee makers
(including Cona), tea pots and gift items.

Suppliers of the finest coffee and tea
to restaurants and hotels.

2 Market Walk
Saffron Walden
☎ (0799) 27130

WE'VE BEEN MAKING SAVINGS SECURE SINCE 1849!

Since then we have grown to one of the largest local Building Societies with assets over £115 million.

However, we have never forgotten our aim of 140 years ago which is to continue to provide a safe place for savings and to offer mortgages for people buying their own home,

Come in and see us today!

HEAD OFFICE:
SAFFRON HOUSE, MARKET STREET,
SAFFRON WALDEN, ESSEX.
TEL: 22211 & 24949

SAFFRON WALDEN
HERTS & ESSEX
BUILDING SOCIETY

Saffron Walden Laundry Co. Ltd.

Commercial & Domestic Launderers & Dry Cleaners

NOT ONLY

A dependable service in all matters of laundry and cleaning.

BUT ALSO

For the sale of top quality bed linen, pillows, continental quilts, towels and bath sets.

13/17 Gold Street, Saffron Walden. Tel: S/W 22588

9 Snowley Parade, Bishop's Stortford. Tel: B/S 92 52128

2 Emson Close, Saffron Walden. Tel: S/W 22588

CHAPTER FIVE

Gold Street

First published in the Saffron Walden Weekly News
27 September – 18 October 1984

Long ago, when Saffron Walden was a tiny, medieval town, a wealthy merchant built himself a fine house on its precincts.

The rich man's servants, passing backwards and forwards to the market place wore a track, parallel to the main street of the town – the High Street. In time the track became a well-worn pathway known as Gowstreet (or Goulstreet) – named after the merchant himself – Simon de Goul.

Sometime between the 17th and 18th centuries Gowlstreet became Gold Street; one of the most important streets in the tightly knit community of old Walden.

Now – no longer a street of artisans and small family businesses – of large families crowded into small houses – where everyone was "Auntie and Uncle" whether related or not – Gold Street has still retained much of its own unique character.

And it would not be unreasonable to assume that No. 53 Gold Street, a house which at one time extended right across the road facing northwards down the hill, was the original-house of Simon de Goul.

Urban and Landscape Designer, Tony Hawkey, has lived at No. 53 for 20 years, and says he believes the actual core of the property dates back to the 16th century, probably earlier.

It is believed to have been the Head Maltsters' house belonging to the Gibson Maltings in the 19th century. But two thirds of the house was destroyed by fire in 1942, when the maltings, then used as a warehouse by Sainsburys, caught fire. (That was the night – they say – rivers of butter ran down the street).

Undoubtedly it was once a rich man's house. And Mr Hawkey, who has been restoring No. 53 gradually for many years, recently found a stylised 18th century fresco over the fireplace in a downstairs room.

A more recent discovery, during re-roofing operations, was, a cat's skeleton found sealed in the chimney. Evidence of the barbaric medieval practice of sealing-up a cat in the chimney to ward off evil spirits and witches.

So, all things considered, it would be quite feasible to suppose that Gold Street originated from this one big house.

Mr Hawkey, a keen conservationist, was one of the original members of the "Save Audley Park Campaign" when it was proposed to build the new sewage treatment works in Audley Park. Now known as the Audley Park Group, it is very much involved in the campaign for saving Swan Meadow.

An ideal time to visit Gold Street is on a Sunday morning. And blessed as it is with a pub at each end, what better excuse for a drink?

Twentieth Century Gold Street starts at the foot of the hill with The Old English Gentleman. However, historically it began with Simon de Goul's house, and so we will stay at the top of the hill, and take a drink at the Sun Inn. But first we must pause to enjoy the fine view of the Church and the lovely old roofs spread out before us.

Ernie Hopkins and his wife Nell have been running the Sun Inn in Gold Street for seventeen years.

East-enders by birth, Ernie was a Turf Accountant in Leigh-on-Sea for many years, but Nell fancied a change.

It had always been her ambition to run a pub, and she realised this when the tenancy of The Sun became vacant. Since moving to Saffron Walden they have loved every minute of their busy working lives.

Friendly, outgoing and warm-hearted, Ernie and Nell make all their customers feel at home straight away. And this includes a cosy fire in the bar when the weather turns chilly. No-one ever feels an outsider. Everyone is included in the conversation whatever the subject.

And you haven't tasted sandwiches until you've tasted Nell's 'doorsteps' as she likes to call them. Freshly cut thick, crusty bread, with plentiful fillings – they are just about the best sandwiches you will find anywhere – and very reasonably priced!

Since their arrival in Saffron Walden, Nell has been an indefatigable worker for charity. And so far she has raised over £140,000 for various good causes.

A former chairman of the Saffron Walden Ladies' Auxiliary; Bishop's Stortford Ladies' Auxiliary, and the Licensed Trade Convalescent homes for the whole of Southern England, as well

Gold Street and the Sun Inn at Cornation time 1911

111

as working for various other local charities, she now has, unfortunately, to restrict her fund-raising to collecting boxes on the bar. Ernie's failing eyesight means she can no longer take on outside activities as much as she used to.

The history of The Sun is not easy to trace. Late 18th century records indicate it was once part of a small maltings. In 1839 it is recorded as "cottage and brewhouse", and not until 1850 does the name 'The Sun' appear in records.

One thing is certain, it never belonged to the Gibsons. Rating lists show that it was bought by Ridleys – the present Brewers – in 1889 – when once and for all it was established as 'The Sun Inn'.

Like No. 53, The Sun suffered considerable damage the night Sainsbury's Maltings caught fire. Nothing now remains of these old maltings, except the name 'Oasthouse Court' – an exclusive complex of late 20th century town houses.

Someone who has recollections of Gold Street when it was still a 'family street' is, Mr Alan Peasgood, who was born at The Sun, during the time his grandparents, Thomas and Emily Overall lived there.

Mr Peasgood, in partnership with his brother, Jack, represents the seventh generation in a family business dating back to 1847. The story of Peasgood the Undertakers is a fascinating saga in itself.

James Day was an Innkeeper at the Queen's Head in the High Street (No. 76) – now a private dwelling and still the family home of the Peasgoods.

Like most 19th century Innkeepers, he did other things as well, including a bit of carpentry and the odd wheelwright's job. Therefore, it was perfectly natural if a friend or member of the family died, to ask James to make up a coffin.

Business prospered. James Day and his son took workshops across the road in one of the cottages which stood on the site where The Friends' Meeting House stands now.

When the cottages were pulled down in 1879 to make way for their new Meeting House, the Society of Friends gave James Day £100 and the materials to build a new workshop. This he built in that part of Gold Street known as Powell's Corner, just across the way from The Sun, and this is the workshop his descendants still use today.

James Day and Herbert Peasgood outside No. 19 in the early days of this century

Generations of the Day family continued to work as carpenters and undertakers until the time came when the last James Day lost his only son at a very early age.

But he had a nephew – Herbert Peasgood – living in the village of Stamford in Lincolnshire. Herbert was one of a very large family so no doubt it was a blessing to his parents when the 18-year-old lad left home to join his uncle in Saffron Walden.

In due course Herbert Peasgood inherited the business from his uncle, and when he died in 1955, his son Reginald took over. Reginald died in 1976 and the business passed to his sons – Alan and Jack.

Both sons had been apprenticed to their grandfather as soon as they left school; but in reality they had entered the family business long before that.

'I have never felt there was anything morbid about being an undertaker,' says Alan Peasgood. 'Jack and I were born into the business. Father was called upon to do all the military funerals during the war, and it was perfectly natural for us to help whenever we could because most of the men had been called-up.

'My most vivid memories are of attending a crash when a German aeroplane came down at Ashdon. I found it terribly exciting. I suppose I was really too young to appreciate the tragedy of the incident at the time.

'After the war father did quite a bit of building in the area, but personally I have no interest in building. Jack and I are both carpenters by trade, and that is what we enjoy most of all, working with wood.'

He continues, 'things have changed enormously since we first entered the business.'

'Grandfather would buy in 'buts' (trees, ready sawn into lengths), and it was our winter job to plane these boards, then stand them in the workshop entrance, which makes a lovely wind-tunnel. From time to time we would turn the wood and brush it down, so that when arrangements came in, the wood was ready for use. Now, for sheer economics we buy in ready-made coffins – time is the most expensive commodity these days.'

'Of course when the maltings were still in operation, there was never any shortage of bearers to shoulder a coffin. The men finished mid-day and were glad of a little extra pay. You had to make sure that everyone got their turn and you did not show favouritism. But now it is extremely difficult to find bearers.'

'Shouldering the coffin is the true country tradition. But even the lightest coffin can become quite a heavy burden after a time. Nevertheless, the men would carry it from the church to the cemetery, with a rest at the top of the common – a trestle for the coffin was put there especially for the purpose.

' On the rare occasions we used horse-drawn carriages, we would hire them from Ben Pledger at the Greyhound.'

All the time we are talking, Jack Peasgood pops in and out of the office. 'Arrangements' have just come in, and things have to be organised. (Undertakers never talk of funerals – always 'arrangements').

When Alan brought out the old account books however, we all became caught up with the fascinating details of those old-fashioned funerals.

Beautiful copperplate handwriting told us that in 1887 the average price of a funeral was £3.7s.6d (£3.36p).

'We think that funerals are expensive these days,' says Alan, 'but when you remember that the average farm-labourer's wage was 10/– (50p) a week – that meant six weeks' wages to pay for a funeral' - so funerals must be cheaper nowadays!'

'Bearers were paid roughly 25p each, sometimes less, and if they were lucky, refreshments were laid on for them.'

One entry in the account books reads, 'refreshments for bearers and undertakers 6/9d. (approx. 30p) Tolling the bell twice 6/– (30p).'

'The bell,' explained Alan, 'would probably have been tolled on the day of death, and on the day of the funeral as well. This was usually done by old Walter Parish, the cemetery custodian.'

Thumbing our way through one book we discover two or three consecutive pages of small entries, each funeral costing exactly 13/– (65p). An epidemic of diphtheria had brought its own deathly toll amongst the children of the the town.

'Now,' says Jack, 'there is one portion of the cemetery completely covered with primroses in the Spring. Someone must have put a clump on one of the children's graves, and they are gradually spreading.'

Although the Peasgoods now buy in ready-made coffins, and the handles are no longer made of solid brass, they still insist on traditional oak and elm.

Nor do they forget that theirs is a highly personalised business. Thankfully, both men have extremely supportive wives who understand that their husbands do not work a nine till five day.

Audrey Peasgood comes from another old-established business family in the town – Gillett's the greengrocers. Whilst Jack's wife Brenda – looks after the financial side of things – is also well aware that being an undertaker's wife means that any sort of regular social life is almost impossible.

'There is a saying in the profession – don't get involved' says Alan Peasgood, 'but you can't help getting involved. A lot of people who call upon us we know personally. And anyway, making funeral arrangements is no ordinary business deal. If you treat it as such, then you are falling short. If clients want to talk, then they must be allowed to talk, and we must be prepared to listen. Our time is their time.'

115

'It is very strange,' he continues, 'we undertakers are always treated as a Music Hall joke. I can't think why, because really people can't do without us. Even at social gatherings you tell someone you are an undertaker and the conversation stops. Then the questions start! People seem to have a morbid fascination with the profession.'

But if you think spending an afternoon in an undertaker's office is morbid, perish the thought! There was a lot of background whistling and banging below stairs, some of it coming from Russell Green, who has worked for the Peasgoods since he left school 35 years ago.

Nor could the tall, good-looking, cheerful young man who reversed my car out of the yard for me, ever be associated in anyway with Musical Hall stereotypes of his profession.

'The Sunday School Outing was always held on August Bank Holiday. One, sometimes two wagons arrived at the Gold Street Meeting Room, clean, with fresh straw on the boards. The horses tails were plaited and decorated, and the drivers were in holiday spirits.

A Gold Street Sunday Outing party about 1907

116

There were baths filled crockery and food, and a bag containing the cricket gear. Mr. Newton – the Sunday School Superintendent – wore a white straw panama hat, attached to his coat with a cord.

We jolted happily on to Gunter's Farm or Thundersley Hall, Wimbish. Mr. Wiseman who owned both farms was there to welcome us.

We quickly alighted from the wagons and rushed to the meadow for games.

The tea was marvellous. I've never tasted such delicious bread and butter and cake since.

When evening shadows began to fall, prize packets, sweets and nuts were given to all the scholars. After this we were again hoisted into the wagons....'

This charming account of a Sunday School outing before 1914 has unfortunately had to be abridged. A great pity – because it is a delightful piece of nostalgia, written from the heart, portraying the simple, unsophisticated pleasures that the children of over 70 years ago enjoyed and children of today seldom experience.

It was written by Miss Lucy Faircloth – who lives in Victoria Avenue – a member of Gold Street Chapel, as her contribution to the Chapel's Centenary Booklet – One Hundred Years of Assembly Witness in Saffron Walden 1870-1970.

Gold Street Chapel stands next door to Peasgoods in Gold Street on a site that was once Freestones Engineering Shop.

The original Assembly was started in 1870 at the Lecture Hall in Hill Street (near to Budgens but now demolished). In 1888 it was moved to Gold Street, to the purpose built Meeting House we know today.

Again, the Centenary Booklet gives the following delightful anecdote about the building of the Chapel:-

'Considerable money had to be borrowed, and it was decided that the money could only be borrowed from members of The Assembly, so that if the Lord returned before the money was repaid, no money would be owing to unbelievers.'

The Centenary booklet, a light-hearted gem of social history, comments on some of the characters of this sincere, outgoing, friendly community with a gentle, kindly humour.

One such story is the tale of the member who lived in Saffron Walden but was always late for the Breaking of Bread on Sundays. This, despite the fact that many members living in the outlying villages walked to the Meetings whatever the weather and were never late.

It was eventually decided to change The Breaking of Bread from 10.30 a.m. to 11.00 a.m. to enable the latecomer to arrive on time. Unfortunately this resulted in the miscreant arriving even later!

Far from being an archaic monument to the past, Gold Street Chapel still survives today as a thriving community of practising Christians. And although the Sunday School Outing is no longer held on August Bank Holiday, starting off with wagons drawn by horses with plaited tails, the Brethren of Gold Street Chapel still provide a great deal of pleasure for a lot of children in and around Saffron Walden.

The Vacation Bible School, started fifteen years ago, is held for one week each August. Housed in large Marquees on the Anglo-American Playing Fields, the school starts each day at 9.30 and goes on until 3.30 with activities such as Bible stories, worksheets, quizzes, arts and crafts and games, and has an average attendance of almost 500 children between the ages of four to fifteen.

Because many children of today no longer go to Sunday School, the Vacation Bible School aims to put over Bible instruction to children in an interesting and relevant way.

In this respect it has proved an undoubted success. Year after year, the same children return to enjoy what has become one of the most popular events of the summer season in Saffron Walden.

The school is run by a team of fifty helpers drawn from churches in the surrounding area, and funded mostly by the Brethren of Gold Street Chapel.

One of the principal founders and organisers of the Vacation Bible School is Mr. Ray Mitson who has been a member of Gold Street Chapel all his life.

Although he was born at No.3 High Street for many years his parents lived at No.19 Gold Street.

His father was Samuel Mitson the sign-writer. He rented No.19 from Cleales the motor engineers because there were

118

plenty of outbuildings at the back of the property and a yard big enough to take any wagon coming in to be painted. (Earlier still, this same property had belonged to James Day the undertaker.)

Next door to the Chapel is No.58, a tiny two bedroomed timber framed cottage dating, like its close neighbours – numbers 56, 54 and 52 – from the late 17th century.

It was here that Alfred Sutton and his wife Emily lived in the early decades of the century.

Alfred Sutton was a Guard on the railway. Many people still recall how he used to stand, whistle in mouth, watching for anyone running down Station Street to catch the train.

He and Emily had 11 children all told, including twins, and they all survived, despite the cramped conditions.

One of them is Miss Alice Sutton, who now lives in Bexhill, but who was born at number 58 Gold Street in 1906. She told me that as she and her brothers and sisters grew up, they moved out of the family home.

'As soon as I left school at the age of 14 I went into Service,' she said. 'My first job was working for an old lady called Mrs. Maggs. She was an old devil!'

'I had quite pretty hair and she used to scrape it all back. She told me if I didn't scrape my hair back I would be a butterfly.'

'She used to make enough porrage to last her a week and keep it in jam-jars.'

'The hours were quite long. I would start at seven o'clock in the morning and finish at six in the evening. I had one Sunday evening off one week, and an afternoon and evening off the next week. But if I stayed in, even if it was my time off, I still had to lay the tray and table.'

Recalling her memories of Gold Street, Miss Sutton said that it was a very happy street, with everyone willing to help one another.

But she also remembered the time an old lady called Sue Adams was put out on to the pavement with all her possessions because she couldn't pay her rent.

'But,' she continued, 'in those days we could play in the street, and we used to have the old jam-jar man around. If you gave him a jam-jar he would give you a paper windmill.'

'Another thing I remember was the Fever Van. I hated it

when it came to collect anyone who had Scarlet Fever. We always used to get a dose of Epsom salts whenever there was fever around.'

'And I remember that when anyone died, the mattress from their bed was taken into the maltings nearby and baked – don't ask me why!'

Alice's brother Percy – born in 1905 – also has vivid memories of living in Gold Street, especially during the First World War when they had four soldiers from the Fifth South Staffordshires billeted on them.

One of the soldiers carved the cap badge of the South Staffordshires on one of the walls of No.58 (it has long since been covered up) and another gave him a cap badge, which he still has in his possession.

He said, 'most of the South Staffs were miners and they made a tremendous fuss of us. One of them came from Nottingham and his parents sent my mother some lace curtains.'

Turn the corner, and we come to No.48 Gold Street, again another late 17th century timber-framed cottage. But to get to it we must lift the latch of the big blue gates which were once a cart-way.

Here, in what was once a courtyard, a small garden with a tiny lawn has replaced the outside privies and communal wash-house – relics of a previous age.

Mrs. Candy Jeffries – a young mother – lives at No.48 but for many people this will always be Alfred Walls the 'snob's' workshop (cobbler). But in 1851 it was the home of James Bass, a journeyman blacksmith.

The next group of cottages – again late 17th century timber-frame – are believed to have been weavers' cottages at one time.

The Norwich crepe industry came to Saffron Walden at the beginning of the 19th century – although it did not last long.

Early prints show women in Gold Street, near to these cottages, stretching lengths of silk crepe across the street.

In 1836 Lord Braybrooke wrote of the many "persons, principally young females" who were employed by the crepe industry. "But the high wages obtained lead to idle and extravagant habits, so that the discontinuance of the work cannot be a matter of regret, and in a short time no one will recollect that it ever existed." (Could it be there was a shortage of servants at Audley End Mansion at that time?).

Straw plaiting was another cottage industry carried out also in this part of the town during the 19th century. This would be an important source of income for many women, reflected by the steady demand for straw for hats.

Numbers 35 to 49 are an interesting terrace of what would appear to be early 19th century red-brick cottages with an intriguing stepped sky-line of red-tiled roofs.

Despite the date 1810 on one of the walls, these cottages are believed to date from 1550 (at least in parts) and assumed to be the Almshouses referred to in the Statutes of the original Saffron Walden Almshouses. And rating lists for 1790 refer to these cottages as Almshouses, but the reason for their rigorous alteration twenty years later has never been disclosed.

Billy and Gladys Mardell live at No.49, in the cottage where Gladys was born 74 years ago.

Gladys was the youngest of ten children, and she still has the chest of drawers which served as her very first cot.

Next door, No.47 is the home of Mrs. Mary Whiteman – author of 'Saffron Walden Portrait of a Market Town'. In 1886 William Bishop the colt-breaker lived here, which is the reason why Mrs. Whiteman is always digging-up horse shoes in her garden!

Mary Whiteman, writer and journalist, came to Saffron Walden fifty years ago with her journalist husband and young family.

Although she herself had grown-up in journalism, and she still did a little part-time freelance writing she says at that time she was mostly involved in bringing up her young family. But it was at this time she joined the Town Library which she found fascinating.

As time progressed she became friendly with the Librarian, Miss E.K. Wakeford, 'who was a scholar and writer, and had a deep appreciation of the contents of the Library,' says Mrs. Whiteman.

When Miss Wakeford's health began to fail, Mary Whiteman assisted her in her work on a voluntary basis, eventually becoming a part-time member of staff for the princely sum of ten shillings (50p) a week.

Miss Wakeford died suddenly 'so naturally I carried on,' Mary says. 'This was at the time they were deciding the future of the Town Library and the fate of the Corn Exchange also, so I held the fort until matters were resolved.'

The outcome of all this was, that Mary found herself employed in the County Library, which was at that time housed in Cambridge House, and far, far away from the old books she so dearly loved.

'I was completely incompetent on the Library counter,' she says, 'and perhaps, because they were glad to get rid of me, I went to work for Mr. Shaw-Ridler on the secretarial side, and I found myself back with the old books once again.

'By this time I realised the wealth of local history which was in the Town Library and which needed to be developed.'

'My husband died in 1974 (he will be remembered by many people as the billeting officer during the Second World War) and I must say, I found working at the Library a tremendous help in enabling me to get over my bereavement.'

'When I retired in 1976 I discovered that I could now come into the Library as an unpaid volunteer, and that was what I wanted. And ever since then I have been involved with the Town Library.'

Many people – myself included – have good cause to feel grateful to Mary Whiteman and her interest in what she calls 'the old books'. Her knowledge of local history is both inexhaustable and valuable and a wonderful source of information for others.

Crossing the street once again, we come to No.40, an early 16th century timber-framed and plastered building, much altered during the 18th and 19th centuries, but still retaining its original jettied front.

Now the D. & M. Fish Bar, it will be remembered by many as John Bacon's Fish Shop. John Bacon bought the premises in 1935 from Walter Housden, painter and plumber, who had been running his business at this address since the turn of the century.

Strangely enough, the previous occupiers of No.40 in the 1890s – Arthur George Courtney and his wife Harriet – were also fish-mongers, so when John Bacon took over, he was reviving a previously established tradition.

The next group of cottages, No.34 to 38 are all part of one early 16th century timber-framed and plastered building, altered sometime during the 18th century, and renovated during the 20th. Again, probably intended as weavers' cottages, they continue the picturesque theme of this lovely old street.

Now we come to numbers 30 and 32, assumed to be late 17th or early 18th century cottages. For many years No.30 was the home of a very wellknown local character – Walter Jarvis.

Walter, who died earlier this year at the age of 86, was born at Cole End, Saffron Walden. His father was a local thatcher and as soon as he left school – before his 14th birthday – Walter became his father's apprentice.

'There was no question of payment,' Walter used to say, 'my father would just give me the odd shilling whenever he felt like it!'

He was almost 15 before he was allowed to thatch a roof himself. And it was always his proud boast that he was taught to thatch properly with real straw – 'not the stuff they use nowadays. Today's straw has too much artificial fertilizer in it. There's no life in it, and it's far too short!'

Walter, his father and his brother Frank, worked all round the Walden area, thatching roofs, slaughtering cattle, selling horses and doing whatever odd jobs came their way. When their father died, Walter and his brother went their separate ways, still thatching, but never trespassing on each other.

Like most of his generation, Walter used to bemoan the passing of the Good Old Bad Old Days.

'They *were* bad old days,' he would say, 'but all the farms were proper farms with bullocks in the yard and cows in the field, and farmers made their farms pay because they had to or they starved.'

He would speak of the time when beer was only twopence a pint, and you could go to the Greyhound (now the Weekly News Office) and get a pint of beer, two-pennyworth of bread and cheese – they gave you the pickle free – a packet of Woodbines and a box of matches, and still get a halfpenny change out of sixpence!

123

Thatcher, Walter Jarvis

Most Saturdays and Sundays, right up until his death, Walter Jarvis could be found in the Railway Arms at lunchtime. An irrepressible character, he had a wealth of salty anecdotes and a fine repertoire of old Suffolk songs, not intended for mixed company.

Legend has it that once, Walter and a certain blacksmith had been doing a spot of celebrating, and returned to the smithy with blacksmith clutching a bottle of rum. Unfortunately the smith fell into the fire and the rum ignited. Walter, with great presence of mind, saved his friend's life by putting out the fire in the most natural way possible!

Walter married Mary Reynolds, a Walden girl, whom he met one August Bank Holiday Monday. Mary herself was also a great character, and was cleaner at the Friends' School for fifty years.

Mary died in the later 1970s, and during her declining years Walter nursed his wife with steadfast devotion.

Before we walk further down the street, a small point of interest is the fact that No.39 (across the road) was once the home of John Evenett, who surely must have been one of Walden's last Town Criers.

In the Almanack for 1903 we find him listed as Bill Poster, but in the 1886 Almanack, John Evenett has a whole half-page advertising himself as "Town Crier and Bill Poster by appointment to the Mayor and Corporation. Sales (auction) attended and assistance rendered on reasonable terms."

The next two cottages, numbers 31 and 33 are 18th century timber-framed and plastered, providing a charming and unprententious contrast to their next-door neighbour No.27.

This handsome 18th century red brick house once belonged to an extensive maltings, believed to have been owned by the Searles. The enormous cart entrance rises through two storeys and joins No.23 – once the maltings office.

No.27 was the home of Vice Admiral Sir Gilbert Stephenson, KBE.,CB.,CMG., during the 1970s.

A sailor of the Old School, who served in sailing ships as a midshipman and fought his first war in 1897 in West Africa, he was, at the age of 62 in the thick of the evacuation of Dunkirk in the Second World War.

His Biography, The Terror of Tobermory, written by

Richard Baker, is an amusing account of a colourful, kindly, but sometimes intimidating character, who could always be relied upon to come up with the unexpected.

He died at the age of 95, but will be remembered as an ardent campaigner for R.A. Butler during the 30s when the Stephensons lived at Springwell Place, Great Chesterford. And later, when he and his daughter, Nancy, lived in Gold Street in the later 1960s as an active member of the Parish Church in Saffron Walden.

At the moment, No.23, the old maltings office, stands as a melancholy shell, slowly disintegrating with neglect.

For two years, Mr. Roy Vincent has been running his Government Surplus business at these premises. But when I spoke to him a few weeks ago, he was on the point of closing down, prior to the sale of the property.

Mr. Vincent is a member of the wellknown Vincent family, whose ironmonger's shop in Church Street became a legend in its comparatively short lifetime (20 years).

Roy has been involved in the Army Surplus business since 1947 when his father started selling military motor cycles. Unfortunately the Church Street shop had to be sold on the death of Mr. Vincent senior, and do-it-yourself enthusiasts have been mourning its passing ever since.

Roy started out on his own at No.23 Gold Street just to see what the potential in Army Surplus was. He has not been disappointed.

A mecca for boys from the ages of 6 to 60 plus, it is a paradise of useful and useless bric-a-brac. Army badges, ammunition pouches, clasp knives, and tin boxes, ideal for hoarders.

As an interim measure, Roy Vincent is carrying on his business on the market on Saturdays until he can find new premises. No easy task, he assured me, with the high cost of shop rents in the town these days.

'High rents have forced a lot of old family businesses to close,' he said. 'Multiple firms from London come into the town and take over because they think the rents are cheap compared to those in London.'

Like a lot of other local shopkeepers, he feels that greedy, out-of-town landlords are killing the character of the town.

Recently Roy Vincent retired from the Saffron Walden Fire

Brigade after over 18 years service. But although he will miss the Fire Brigade, he intends to continue with his activities in the St. John Ambulance Association, which he has belonged to for 28 years.

——— · ———

Numbers 19 and 21 are an early 19 century plain red brick house, not without a certain amount of restrained elegance to be found in architecture of this period.

Now a publishing office, No. 19 was once the home of James Day, great-grandfather of Alan and Jack Peasgood. The yard at the back of the house, which he used as his carpenter's shop, was the same yard that later, Mr. Samuel Mitson the signwriter used.

No. 24 is yet another old maltings, now occupied by the Unemployment Benefit Office on one side of the cart entrance and a builder's office on the other side. For almost 100 years these premises have been associated with Myhill & Sons, Corn Merchants.

Ernest Rushmere and Ernie junior with a converted model T Ford

127

Alderman Addy Nunn Myhill will be remembered by many people as a former Mayor of the town (1917/18) and Honorary Freeman of the Borough (December 1919). His son, Captain Henry Thurgood Myhill, also served the town as Councillor during the early 1930s.

Tracing back the history of No.24 however, my earleist records show that in 1790, it was a maltings owned by Mrs. Sarah Edwards, a widow, who presumably took over from her husband.

By 1815 however, the maltings were owned by Stephen Robinson, who worked them until the late 1830s when the property was bought by John Archer who rented it first to John Parish, then James Richards, and finally William Chalk.

William Chalk appears to have bought the property from John Archer in 1850, but I can find no indication as to whether it was still a maltings at that time

Descriptions in the rating lists vary. Sometimes it is described as cottage, stable and warehouse, and at others, house yard and buildings.

Thomas Chalk (William's son?) must have sold the property to Myhill's in 1886.

——— · ———

Perhaps the most important industrial feature of 20th century Gold Street is the Saffron Walden Laundry Company.

Again, another old-established family firm, bought by Mr. Gerald Southall in 1897, it is now run by his grandson, Mr. Gerald Southall junior, together with his mother, Mrs. Eileen Southhall, his aunt Mrs. Jill Griffiths and her son, Stephen.

Many people will remember Mr. Gerald's father, Mr. Jack Southall, who died in 1978. He was a kind, and generous employer, remembered with affection by many of his old employees.

It was during his time as Managing Director in 1961, that a fire completely gutted the Laundry. But it was thanks to his enterprise and leadership, that the Laundry never stopped trading and none of the workers were laid off.

Work was farmed out to other laundries, who rallied round to help their competitor, and alternative sorting and packing

Fire at Saffron Walden Laundry – photo David Campbell

arrangements were found temporarily. And so within a comparatively short-time a brand new laundry stood on the site of the old one.

Although Saffron Walden Laundry has its roots firmly planted in the past, all equipment and techniques used are extremely modern. Nevertheless, a high standard of handwork is still required in order to achieve a super quality finish.

The Laundry employs approximatley 50 people, many of whom have been with the company since they left school.

Seventy-five year-old May for instance, who lived in East Street with her grandmother in the early 1920s and went to work at the Laundry when she was 14½.

Her first job was shaking out the clothes as they came from the big washing machines. After a week of this she was allowed to feed the Calendar (a long machine which ironed all the flat pieces like tea-towels and table linen).

At first she hated the job because it was so noisy, but gradually she got used to it, and worked her way up to become a supervisor, staying until she retired at the age of 68.

In those early days the hours were long – from 8 o'clock in the morning until 6.30 in the evening. No-one had a fixed job, and everyone tried their hand at everything. But she says they were a great bunch of girls and she made lots of friends.

'We took great pride in our work. And Mrs. Dolly Southall used to say – you are experts, but I have made you so!'

Although laundry methods have become technically more sophisticated over the years, and now only one hand-ironer is employed where once there were four; and the "glad-iron" (a huge, heavy iron on a pulley, heated by gas) is no longer used for starched work, the number of staff has decreased only slightly.

A landmark of Gold Street in the 1920s was James Freeman's furniture shop, which stood in front of the old laundry. Long since gone, it is still remembered by the older generation.

Next door to the Laundry, and an integral part of it, stands the Laundry House, sometimes referred to as "Gabriel Harvey's House."

This is No.13 Gold Street, a 16th century timber-framed and plastered building, with a stone panel inserted in its 20th century chimney-stack showing the date 1565 and the initial J.H.–A.H. (John and Alice Harvey). These initials are repeated on the bressumer beam supporting the jettied upper storey at the front of the building.

John Harvey was a wealthy Saffron Walden rope-maker who had three sons, Gabriel, Richard and John.

He built himself a fine house in the Market Place as well as the one in Gold Street.

All his sons were educated at the Grammar School in Castle Street, and later Gabriel went to Cambridge where he became Professor of Rhetoric and a good friend of the poet Edmund Spenser.

After his retirement from Trinity Hall in 1598, Gabriel came back to Walden, and it is generally assumed that he spent the last 30 years of his life at No.13 Gold Street.

During the latter years of his life he devoted much time to developing an apple, which is still in existence today. Yellowish green in colour, with minute black spots on the skin, poor in flavour and keeping, it is said to be very good for making mincemeat and cider.

Recently, Mr. Peter Cox of Nottingham University has revived an interest in the apple, and a two year-old sapling was planted in Mrs. Mary Whiteman's garden (No.47). This year (1984) the young tree has borne fruit for the first time.

In the 1920s, Ernest Rushmer, a farmer from Sewards End, brought his family to live at No.13.

His farm, like most farms in those days was small and mixed and included a dairy herd. Ernest however, more enterprising than his neighbours, decided to specialise. He took some of his milk to Saffron Walden to sell, and realised there was an opening for starting a milk delivery round.

So he moved to Gold Street, bought a horse and cart (eventually replaced by a Tin Lizzie); collected milk from the surrounding farmers, processed it and delivered it locally.

One of his earliest delivery boys was a wellknown local character – Stanley Wilson – former Mayor and Distinguished Citizen of Saffron Walden.

After a short spell in Gold Street, Ernest moved to King Street (No.12) and then in 1929 moved back to Gold Street, to Dolphin House.

131

Dolphin House is a picturesque 17th century timber-framed and plastered building, altered in the 18th century with a mid-19th century addition. Believed to have been an old coaching inn at one time, it has 22 rooms and a fine open staircase.

It is now the home of Fred and Iris Rushmer. Fred is the youngest of Ernest's five children, and runs the ACR Dolphin Taxi Service. Iris has her own enterprise – The Dolphin Wool Shop.

Now we come to The Old English Gentleman, a typical English country-town pub, low ceilinged, oak beamed, warm and friendly.

The late Sam Mitson, sign-writer with Fred Rushmer's step brother

The licensees, Richard and Anne Hewlett have only been running the pub for a few months, but have already made it an outstanding success, despite the fact that neither of them had ever worked in a pub before. Richard was an electrician and Anne worked in a clothes boutique.

Records show that The Old English Gentleman was a "House and Baking Office" in 1839, and continued thus until about 1850.

In 1856 it is recorded as a "Beerhouse" owned or rented by Thomas Brown who carried on until 1886. And it was only in 1893, when Joseph Penning took over, that the name The Old English Gentleman appears in the rating lists.

The corner of Gold Street dominated by the wall of Budgen's Supermarket, was once the site of The Co-op Drapery and Outfitting Department, but older people will remember it as the home of the Saffron Walden Liberal Club.

Going back to 1869 however, we find that Joseph Travis the "Naturalist" had his shop at No.1 Gold Street. This would have been one of the cottage properties pulled down at the beginning of this century.

In one of these cottages, according to Gladys Mardell, there lived an old woman reputed to have been a witch. Whether she was or not no-one can say, but she dressed all in black and wore a tall, witch-like hat, and frightened all the young girls.

Next door to Joseph Travis's shop lived Walter Francis the Boot and Shoe Maker who, in his advertisement in the 1886 Almanack "begged to call attention to his special line in hand-made water-tights!"

But the Census of 1850 records "The British Girls' School" as being somewhere on or near this site, and as far back as 1839 "House and School-room" appear in the rating lists year after year. Although the earliest records use the word "Academy".

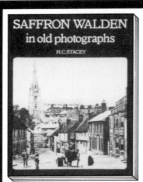

THREE BOOKS FOR THOSE WHO LOVE SAFFRON WALDEN

Saffron Walden In Old Photographs £4.95- Photo's of the Town and it's people during the last 100 years.
Portrait of a Market Town £1.50- The historical guidebook.
A Pictorial Guide £3.95- Superb colour photographs of local attractions.
" These books should be read before a visit, consulted during a visit and relished afterwards."
Available from:

THE C·W·DANIEL COMPANY LTD

——— PUBLISHERS ———
1 CHURCH PATH · SAFFRON WALDEN
ESSEX CB10 1JP · ENGLAND
TELEPHONE 0799 ·21909

CHAPTER SIX

Little Walden Road

First published in the Saffron Walden Weekly News
October 25 – November 1 1984

It must have been very pleasant to walk along Little Walden Road at the turn of the century.

The air would have smelled sweeter and fresher, and the noise of the birds would have deafened your ears, not the noise of the traffic. The fields, on either side of the road would have been smaller, and the hedges and trees more plentiful.

Starting out on your way northwards to Little Walden you might have stopped first to fortify yourself at the Victory pub.

Low-ceilinged, cosy and welcoming, the Victory was built in the early 19th century. Its foundations, however, are obviously much older, with the familiar brick arches and flint walls of many Saffron Walden cellars

Twenty-five years ago, the bones of a young girl were discovered when part of the cellar was being opened-up. No foul-play was suspected, the bones were proved to be centuries old, and assumed to be part of some mystic gypsy ritual.

The Landlord, Alan Batchelor, says quite definitely that the cellar is haunted. Neither of his two dogs will go anywhere near it – but the cat loves it!

Alan and his wife Diane came to the Victory in 1976. Up until then Alan had been a National Accounts Manager in what he terms "The Booze Trade". It was a job which involved travelling over 50,000 miles each year, keeping him away from home for long stretches at a time, with the result he hardly ever saw Diane and his two daughters.

When the opportunity came along to run the Victory, he grasped it with both hands.

Cellar at the Victory reputed to be haunted

'We thought it had great potential' says Alan, 'and we loved the town and the people.'

During the eight years that the Batchelors have been running the pub they have integrated themselves wholeheartedly into the life of the town in many different ways.

This includes many lively fund-raising events such as Crisp Throwing Contests; Drag Walks and Diane's entry into the Mayor's mini-marathon. Everyone joins in the fun and no matter what happens – it's all for a good cause. One of which is the £1,000 they raise each year for a Guide Dog for the Blind.

Adjacent to the Victory is Upper Square, one of the few Squares and Courts belonging to Castle Street which still remains. It is here that, over 60 years ago, the Flea Factory stood.

'It wasn't a Flea Factory dear,' says 87 year-old Mrs. Rosetta Johnson, 'it was The Skin Factory. There weren't any fleas!'

Mrs. Johnson should know. From the age of 11 until after she married she worked at the Skin Factory in Upper Square.

She was born in Littlebury, the daughter of a carpenter and one of nine children. Every morning she left her home at Littlebury at a quarter-past-six and walked to Walden to be at the Factory for a quarter-to-seven.

'Sometimes,' she says, 'I would get up at 4 o'clock in the morning to do the washing for my mother, because she had three young children under three years old.'

Horrifying tales have been told about The Skin Factory, about the fleas, the maggots and the smell. But Mrs. Johnson told me that all the skins came from London, fully cured and as stiff as boards. They did not smell, nor were there any fleas or maggots.

The Factory was an old house, now demolished, with the lower rooms knocked into one large area. Five girls spent their working day scraping the fur off the skins. The money was good, and so was the Boss.

But sometime in the early 1920s the Skin Factory was closed, probably as a result of the slum clearance scheme which was just taking place about that time.

The teeming, swarming mass of warm-hearted humanity which formed the life-blood of Castle Street, began to be systematically up-rooted and housed in modern houses and flats, first along Little Walden Road, and then later, during the 30s, down nearby Catons Lane.

Mrs. Johnson was one of these, and now she lives at No.6 Catons Lane.

Eighty-two year-old Sidney Barker, who now lives at No.1 Upper Square, was another whose family was rehoused at this time.

He told me he was born in Middle Square, one of nine children – five boys and four girls. And when Middle Square was pulled down the family went to live at No.5 Little Walden Road.

He said that in the old days there were 22 houses in Upper Square. Now, there are only three houses left.

'There used to be a big wash-house up near the Victory where our mothers used to do the washing and then they would take it to dry on the Common.'

'My father was a builder's labourer, and when I left Castle Street School at the age of 12 – because the First World War had started – I went to look after a pony for an old lady in Ashdon Road.'

Later, Mr. Barker married his childhood sweetheart, Victoria Cornell, who also lived in Castle Street.

In 1929 he became a driver for Haslers the Corn Merchants where he worked for 32 years. Not only did he drive the lorry but he had to lug the sacks as well.

'A sack of oats would weigh 12 stones, and a sack of barley 16 stones; wheat 18 stones; beans 19 stones and clover seed 20 stones. And the sacks themselves weighed 4 lbs.'

'Yes, they were hard working days, but they were good living days, and I enjoyed my work, no doubt about that!'

Before we continue on our way along Little Walden Road, we will turn left and walk down Catons Lane as far as Catons Lane Farm. This is now the home of Mr. and Mrs. Ketteridge, who have lived at the Farm for over 20 years.

The farm was built in 1831, and in the latter part of the 19th century it was hired by William Caton, the son of John Caton the cow-keeper at Cinder Hall. And what had hitherto been known as Lofts Lane, became Catons Lane.

About a hundred years ago, a young man by the name of

David Gillett started a little market garden somewhere near here. He was the great-grandfather of Mr. Maurice Gillett, and founder of the old-established family business – Gillett's the greengrocers.

Returning to Little Walden Road once again we cross over to the east side and pause to admire No.2, an 18th century timber-framed and plastered house. In 1851 Henry Beans a rope-maker lived here.

A few yards further along we come to the Pound, a small brick enclosure, slightly crumbling with a gateway opening on to the road.

A plaque on the wall of the Pound explains that "this Ancient Pound provided temporary accommodation for stray animals caught in the town. A fee was paid to the local police to redeem them."

The Pound dates back to the 18th century when Common-right Holders were allowed to graze their animals on the Common, and all too frequently these rights were abused by others. (Animals allowed to graze on the Common had to be branded with their owner's mark).

An official called "The Pinder" was appointed to round up stray or illegally grazing animals, impound them, and collect the fines.

Pounds were usually of two different kinds "overt" (open to the sky like this one) used for animals, and "covert" (roofed in, used for goods distrained for rent or damage).

There are few Pounds in existence today, and Saffron Walden is extremely lucky to have such a fine example.

Walking along toward the open country, we pass The Green on the left-hand side of the road. This is a complex of small flats, another part of the Castle Street re-housing scheme.

On the right-hand side of the road are a handsome pair of 19th century brick and flint cottages with unusually patterned tiled roofs.

———— · ————

A feature of Little Walden Road for many years has been the Chalk Pit. But by 1975 the Chalk Pit had been virtually worked out and two local business men, Mr. Frank Brooke and Mr. Peter Price, both keen golfers, decided to turn it into a Golf Driving Range.

The pit was filled in with old cars, perambulators and what-have-you, covered with a layer of top soil and grassed over. Then, driving distances of 25 yard intervals were marked out, so that experts and beginners might practise or perfect their golf swing.

Mrs. Joyce Smith, who lives in one of the cottages near to the Golf Range has a long standing connection with the old Chalk Pit.

It was her father, Percy Cornell, who, when he was a young lad, helped load the lime-kilns for Mr. Tatham, the lime-burner.

Samuel Tatham rented the pit from one of the Gibsons in the late 1880s. (Probably Edmund Birch Gibson who owned most of Little Walden).

Joyce's mother, Mrs. Lilian Cornell, also said that once there were several drinking wells on the site of the Chalk Pit very much in use at the turn of the century.

As we leave the Golf Range, the town recedes gently to make way for the open countryside and simultaneously we reach two farm tracks, one on either side of the road.

Eastwards is the track to Byrd's Farm and across the road is the lane we follow to Westley Farm.

Westley is the home of Martin and Suzanne Duke and their three young sons. It is a fine old farmhouse dating back to Tudor times.

Martin's father, Mr. Richard Duke, bought the farm in 1948, but Martin has been cultivating Westley's 800 acres for the past 14 years.

Like many old houses, Westley Farm is reputed to be haunted. Suzanne and Martin say they have never seen the ghost, but Mr. Richard Duke insists he has.

The ghost is that of Mrs. Spicer, the wife of William Spicer, a previous farmer, who continued to live in the house long after her husband died.

During the time Richard Duke lived at Westley, the drinks were kept in a corner cupboard in the living room. And, Mr. Duke swears that, on more than one occasion he saw the living room door open of its own accord. Then, the door of the drinks cupboard would open slowly, after which a chilly presence passed through the room, opening another door at the far end, and slowly one door after another throughout the house could be heard opening. (Mrs. Spicer helping herself to a drink?)

'You must remember there would have been no electricity only candles and oil lamps in those days,' says Martin. (William Spicer was farming Westley in 1886).

'The track leading to the farm would have been muddy and unmade, virtually impassable in winter, and it must have been a very lonely life for her.'

Martin assured me that once the corner cupboard was removed, the ghost was never seen or heard again.

Returning to the main road once more, we eventually arrive at Cinder Hall.

Cinder Hall is a Victorian folly of immense charm, resplendent with Dutch Gable, Gothic window, turret and battlement – a riot of architectural achievement.

Cinder Hall

Dating back to the early 19th century, it is a unique example of one man's dream. Love it; hate it; you cannot remain indifferent to Cinder Hall!

Little is known about its origins. The name is derived from the cinder facings on the brick and flint walls, which form an unusual and decorative treatment.

Mr. Kenneth Mark, a local architect specialising in design for restoration and extensions of old buildings, feels the pattern is extremely interesting. 'Particularly the decoration on the south elevation. It is almost before its time. There is a strong feeling of Art Nouveau about it.'

Mr. Mark, whose son Peter, bought Cinder Hall a few years ago, designed the plans for the enlargement and modernisation of the house.

He believes that at one time the original building must have been much larger and that it was probably quite a substantial farmhouse in its day. And possibly, the builder was his own architect and built Cinder Hall for his own use.

He says he was quite surprised to see the excellent condition of the cinders decorating the walls which showed no sign of deterioration.

But extending and restoring a Victorian folly was no easy task. The very nature of Cinder Hall's unorthodox design demanded unorthodox yet sympathetic treatment. Cinder infills had to be fitted in by hand; windows especially made, and original features adapted to modern needs. The end result is a charming blend of 19th century capriciousness and 20th century practicality.

Unfortunately, Peter Mark, an Ealing building contractor, found Cinder Hall too far away from his work to make commuting comfortable, and so reluctantly put the house on the market.

Meanwhile Cinder Hall remains, sublime and mellow, a romantic fantasy in a pedestrian world.

A little further along, still on the west side of Little Walden Road, stands Mead Hall. Again an early 19th century house, forerunner of its kind, built when the town began to gradually creep outwards into the countryside, and named after the field on which it was built – Long Mead.

142

INDEPENDENT

SINCE 1825

AUCTIONEERS

ESTATE AGENTS

THE
CAMBRIDGE
SALEROOM

IS THE
AUCTION CENTRE
FOR EAST ANGLIA

For expert advice and help
phone our
Saleroom Department
2 Clifton Road
OFF CHERRY HINTON ROAD

Cambridge CB1 4BW
Telephone 0223-358721

OVER
160 YEARS
EXPERIENCE

**For friendly, personal advice
contact the Independent
Property Professionals**

49/53 Regent Street Cambridge CB2 1AF
Tel 0223 358721

25 Market Place Ely Cambs CB7 4NP
Tel 0353 662266

8 Hill Street Saffron Walden Essex CB10 1JD
Tel 0799 23656

11B Churchgate Street Soham Cambs CB7 5DS
Tel 0353 722777

Meldreth House Wellington Street Newmarket
Suffolk CB8 0HT Tel 0638 663228

CHEFFINS GRAIN & ◀◀◀ COMINS

REGISTERED
HOUSE BUILDER

JOHN BROWN
(SAFFRON WALDEN) LIMITED

Builders of

Quality Houses of Distinction

Completed Houses Available for Immediate Possession in Various Districts

Select Plots Usually Available For Houses To Client's
Requirements

CASTLE HILL
SAFFRON WALDEN
Telephone
Saffron Walden
(0799) 23335

144

CHAPTER SEVEN

Castle Street

First published in the Saffron Walden Weekly News
November 8 1984 - January 24 1985

Castle Street! The most picturesque street in Saffron Walden.
A charming jumble of mainly medieval cottages.

Fifty or sixty years ago, perhaps not even as far back as that,
these cottages - many just two rooms up, two rooms down,
were despised, rejected and all too often demolished. Now
they are an estate agent's dream, much sought after and
prized.

In the middle of the 1920s a vast slum clearance scheme
uprooted the teeming warm-hearted community that was
Castle Street and rehoused them in smart, modern council
houses.

Bureaucracy gave them a chance in life, and at the same
time robbed them of companionship and a sense of belonging. Never again were the people of Castle Street to experience the comforting feeling of comradeship which so often
springs from adversity.

How did it all happen? Why did one of the oldest and
probably most prosperous streets in Saffron Walden become
the town's most notorious slum?

Castle Street, like High Street, and Church Street, started as
an earth track leading from the early Saxon church and
fortress.

The original castle which gave the street its name has long
since disappeared. The present ruins, high on the top of the
hill near the Common, are the remains of the 12th century
fortress built by Geoffrey de Mandeville - a 40ft square keep
with fragments of wall.

The steep banks in the back gardens on the southern side of

145

Castle Street are due to the alignment of the houses along the earlier castle walls.

In 1620 Castle Street boasted 61 buildings - more than any other street in the town. In addition it had a school, tithe barn and malt-mill. If records are correct, it would therefore appear that Castle Street was one of the most important streets in the town at that time.

But in 1757 the first signs of crowding appear. Large houses were sub-divided to make several smaller ones. Agricultural tenements were made into courts and squares, a tendency which grew rapidly throughout the 19th century, resulting in the properties declining in rateable value.

So the poorest people in the town came to live in the small cottages and crowded courts of Castle Street, and by 1880, 230 separate dwellings were recorded and overcrowding was at its worst.

But the very poverty and overcrowding that dragged Castle Street down to become the town's most notorious slum, saved it from the despoiling fingers of the developers.

No rich man wanted to build himself a fine Georgian mansion amongst the teeming masses of Castle Street. No Victorian entrepreneur paraded his wealth in many-gabled Gothic brick. Castle Street was left strictly alone.

So although the slum clearance of the 20s and 30s of this century swept away many of the tiny squares and courts, Castle Street has still managed to retain much of its original character, in outward appearances at least.

Only a fool would mourn the passing of the communal outside privies and wash houses. The medieval architecture loses much of its picturesque charm when its walls, mouldering with damp, become a haven for vermin.

It is hard to keep up standards when even the most elementary forms of hygiene are difficult to maintain. But the people who occupied these hovels had no choice, they were poor, and all too often victims of avaricious landlords.

Nevertheless, amongst all the dirt and desperation there were many honest, law-abiding citizens who cherished their self-respect and took pride in their humble homes. Yet, when the time came to relinquish them, they left without regret.

The cottages which remained standing in Castle Street

were eventually snapped up by a new generation who did not associate lath and plaster with poverty and dirt. Brought up in an entirely different environment they found the crumbling cottages aesthetically and historically pleasing and set about renovating them.

It has been said that in 1850 there were 30 beerhouses in Castle Street, yet records of 1860 show only six public houses (seven if you count the Victory) and one maltings.

True, there was a lot of drunkenness in Castle Street in the latter half of the 19th century, but drunkenness was prevalent all over the country at that time, and not just amongst the working classes.

The 1851 Census List gives us some idea of the type of people who lived in the Street at that time. Often there were ten or twelve people, sometimes more, in the tiny cottages.

There was a goodly sprinkling of artisans, many with their own businesses - blacksmiths, tanners, rope-makers - shopkeepers were plentiful too. There was also a farmer and an iron-founder, a solicitor's clerk and a solicitor and several other clerks as well.

Skills, requiring creative ability long since lost are also in evidence, Betsy Bird, the straw bonnet maker, and Mary Ann Morgan, the 23 year-old button maker, added their contribution to the talents of his heterogeneous mass of humanity.

Children abounded, and the average age of the adults was astoundingly low. Death would have been a frequent and, perhaps sometimes, a blessed visitor to many of these humble homes.

There would have been plenty of filth, flies and fleas. In the 19th century there were no motor vehicles until the latter decade, and dunghills would have been common - and fleas. Even wealthy Quakers could have fleas.

But, taking everything into consideration, it is the colourful characters who lived in Castle Street in the late 19th century and the early decades of the 20th who turned the street into a legend.

'I used to know a lot of the shady characters who lived in Castle Street,' says 95 year-old Len Dix of Windmill Hill.

'My grandfather had the Cement Works in West Road and

employed most of them. I worked in the office and I had to pay the men on Saturdays when they knocked-off at one o'clock.

'They called Castle Street the East End of Saffron Walden in those days. There were always fights - real fights - on Saturday nights. And a lot of the men never turned up for work on Mondays.'

Mr. Dix speaks of the time when he was walking through one of the wards of Addenbrookes Hospital in Trumpington Street, Cambridge, many years ago, and was hailed by a familiar voice from one of the beds. Only the eyes and mouth were visible, the rest of the man was covered in bandages, but young Len recognised the voice of "Sixey" when he heard it.

Sixey was a Castle Street character, small in stature, with a frequent inclination to drown his sorrows in drink. Unfortunately on this particular occasion his wife had objected and set about him with the poker.

Police sergeant Dick Crickmore lives on in the memories of many people, because it is said he was the only policeman who dared to walk down Castle Street alone in the early decades of the century.

One of his successors was a constable nicknamed "Clap-clop" who must have patrolled Castle Street in the late 30s and who, according to Mrs. Rosetta (Polly) Johnson, could soon settle any dispute when necessary.

"Monkey Start" seems to be remembered by everyone. Stanley Wilson, writing in "Saffron Crocus" calls him the "Samson of the City - a heavy man of over six feet, who could carry 3 cwt of cement, one sack over his shoulders and one under each arm!"

We will learn more about these and other characters as we walk along the street.

In the meantime, the spirit of Castle Street is best illustrated by two much-loved District Nurses, now retired, Katherine Lambert and Margaret Anderson, who pedalled their way up and down the street on their bikes during the terrible winter of 1946-47, when the whole of the town was virtually crippled with a flu epidemic.

They say, 'conditions were dreadful. Everything was still

rationed and the people in the old houses in Castle Street couldn't get enough fuel to warm their homes.

'But they were so good to each other. If there was a young baby in a house, you only had to go from neighbour to neighbour begging a bit of coal here and a bit of wood there - they would do anything to help each other out.

'About this time, a young girl gave birth to an illigitimate baby boy in a lavatory one cold winter's morning. The baby was ten weeks premature, and there was no chance of getting it into hospital.

'But the whole of Castle Street rallied round to help, and we got the most marvellous co-operation from everyone.

'Now that boy is a father himself, but he owes his life to the wonderful people of Castle Street.'

Step over the threshold of Salmons' Shop at No.1 Castle Street and take a step backwards in time, to the time when an old-fashioned penny went a long way, and even a half-penny spent wisely, could buy quite a lot.

Ever since 1908 this tiny general store has been run by the Salmon family.

Salmon's General Stores

In those days of course, they would have sold practically everything. Paraffin for the lamps which lit the houses; candles for the bedrooms; Zebo for the kitchen range; ham cut from the bone and flour from the sack.

Smiling faces advertising forgotton goods still line the walls of the shop, and on the counter the old-fashioned brass scales still stand together with a colourful row of jars containing sweets. And one knows instinctively that the unexpected can be found here.

The actual building itself, which includes No.3 next door, dates back to the early 16th or 17th century.

Timber-framed and plastered, its brick front belongs to the early 19th century. Wings on either side, extending north-wards, hint that at one time this might have been an early Hall House. And on one of the richly carved twin gables at the front, the initials I.W. 1843 can be seen.

Records dating 1821 state that a Boulting Mill stood on this site. (Boulting cloths were meshed clothes used instead of the original haircloths for the drying processes in the malting industry). This therefore, would have been an important industry considering the number of maltings in the town at that time.

The decline of the malting industry progressed with the 19th century, and in 1851 the name John Wills, cooper, appears in the rating list for this property. From this we may suppose that he converted the Boulting Mill into two properties.

Again, Nos. 5 and 7 Castle Street were once all one building, and are believed to be much earlier than their 18th century plastered front.

Listed as a beerhouse and stables –Landlord, William Elson – in 1869, the bracket for the beerhouse sign may still be seen hanging from the timber-board gable of No.5. This was not, as is generally supposed, The Bell public house – that was higher up the street.

Behind the premises stood a blacksmith's shop. The blacksmith, Charles Chamberlain, later moved to George Street, but the remains of his old furnace may still be seen in the garden behind No.5.

No.5 is now the home of Mrs. Jill Cranwell. Mrs. Cranwell

whose maiden name was Saville, was born at Langley and went to school at Arkesden.

She has been living at No.5 Castle Street for over 30 years, and is wellknown for her expertise in judging the domestic cookery competitions at local horticultural and village shows.

She herself is a professionally qualified cook, and was, for many years, manageress of "Ye Auld Hoose" Hotel (now the Saffron Hotel).

No.7 was once the home of the Yorkshire-born authoress, Christine Dennison Smith, who died some years ago.

Now let us cross the road and pause to enjoy the unique feature of the Roman Catholic Church, which was created from a barn once belonging to the The Close (the 15th century house which once belonged to Francis Gibson).

About the turn of the century, a wealthy parson, newly converted to the Roman Catholic Faith, bought The Close. His name was Father Charles Rose Chase.

At the expense of a member of the Catholic Missionary Society, the barn belonging to the house was converted into a Church and opened for worship in 1906.

But it was not until 1910 that there was a permanent priest for The Church of Our Lady of Compassion.

The present Parish Priest is Father Mayston. A Londoner by birth, he has been in Essex since 1968 - the last eight years spent in Saffron Walden.

Father Mayston assured me that these have been very, very happy years, saying, 'it is the only country parish I have been in where you are recognised within a few years. It is such a very friendly town, and all the churches work together so well.'

It has been assumed for a number of years that the original barn was a tithe barn for the Vicar of Walden. But J.G. O'Leary, writing in the Saffron Walden Antiquarian Society's Journal, says he can find no evidence of this.

Next door to the Roman Catholic Church is the Pentecostal Church. Inaugurated in 1936, and originally the laundry building belonging to The Close, it once served as the Parish Room to the Catholic Church.

On the other side of The Church of Our Lady of Compassion stands Trinity House. This is a late 17th or early 18th century timber-framed and plastered building, refronted in 1846 with grey gault brick.

Looking back through old rating lists, we find that this was the home of the Rev. Francis Norgate, who appears to be the first permanent Roman Catholic Priest to reside in Saffron Walden.

Later, No.27 across the road became the Presbytery, until the present one was built during the 1930s.

Trinity House is now the home of Dr. and Mrs. Boyes-Smith, who told me that at one time a flight of steps in the corner of their garden led to a right of access into the Churchyard. The right of access has long since been rescinded, but it does give rise to speculation about the name "Trinity House".

Nos. 4 and 6, next door to Trinity House, now known as "Flemings", will be familiar to many domestic pets in and around Saffron Walden.

For many years this picturesque 15th century timber-framed building has been associated with a local veterinary practice - from whence comes the name.

But what is Flemings for some, is "Silletts" to others. Speak of Silletts to any of the older generation in Saffron Walden and they are sure to exclaim 'Silletts' puffs!'

Mrs. Marjorie Sutton, whose Maiden name was Cornell, lived in and around Castle Street until she married, and remembers Silletts well, especially their puffs!

'We would queue up very early on cold winter mornings for hot puffs, and when we got them home, mother would split them open and spread them with margarine or dripping.

'Oh - they were out of this world! I don't know how much they cost, but mother always had enough money to buy Silletts' puffs!'

John Sillett was a baker and it was he who started the first Co-op Bakery in Walden at No.51 Ashdon Road. Later, in 1910, he decided to branch out on his own and bought No.4 Castle Street from George Balls.

Records show that Nos. 4 and 6, have always been a baker's shop. So it is quite possible that John Sillett was buying one of the longest established businesses in the town at that time.

Because it stood next door to the Wheatsheaf public house,

Mrs Nan Sillett in the doorway of her shop

John called his bakery "The Wheatsheaf Bakery". But the name never really caught-on - everyone preferred to call it Silletts.

John died at the early age of 51. None of his sons had entered the family business but, Stanley, who was at that time working for Adams & Land the solicitors, gave up his job and took up the reins.

Unfortunately for everyone, Stanley was called-up during the Second World War, and so the family business had to close down.

Stanley is now dead, but his brother Leslie, now 73, and sister Peggy, 75, are still living in Walden. Leslie became an estate agent, and eventually a partner in the wellknown firm of Watsons.

He told me that his father usually owned two horses to pull their bread carts, and these were housed in the stables behind the shop (now a delightful cottage standing in the grounds of Flemings).

'One of our horses, Kitty the mare, was very well known. We had her in the very early twenties and she was a superb trotter! She could go really fast!

'It was my job to take the horse and cart down to the pool in Swan Meadow in summer time and stand the wheels of the cart in the water.

'The heat made the wheels shrink and the tyres fall off, so it was necessary to make the wood swell again to hold the tyres in place.

'In winter I would take the horses round to Mr. Coe the blacksmith in Church Street (now Cleales) to have their shoes roughened so they wouldn't slip on the icy roads.'

As a matter of curiosity I asked Mr. Sillett how much their puffs were to buy.

'A penny each (real money),' he said, 'but you must remember, you got an awful lot for your money, they were a meal in themselves!'

The Wheatsheaf Inn, now No.8 Castle Street, ceased to be a public house sometime between 1901 and 1911, and since that date has always been a private residence. Constructed of plain grey gault brick, it is believed to date from the early 19th century.

Next door a pleasant row of tiny 18th century timber-framed and plaster cottages - Nos.10 to 14 - add contrast to No.8's somewhat restrained architecture. So also does No.16, Church House, which dates from the late 18th or very early 19th century.

Across the road we find No.9, recorded as early 16th century; whilst Nos.11 and 13, were once all one 17th century building.

Like so many Castle Street cottages No.11 has a delightfully Dickensian bow window, harking back to the early 19th century. Here, Allen Taylor had his fishmonger's shop from about 1876 until 1901.

The Almanack for 1886 lists Taylor as being one of the two most important fishmongers in the town, with another shop in Market Street. (The other fishmonger was Hardwicks).

Nos.15, 17 and 19 are all late 17th or early 18th century buildings, and according to records, No.15 was originally an addition to Nos.17 and 19 (all one house).

154

Interesting features of No.19 are the ornate 19th century bargeboards to the gabled cross-wing; the iron lattice casements and the shallow oriel window; all characteristics of the Pugin influence on architecture at this time, but unusual for Castle Street.

No.19 stands on the corner of a small alleyway leading into Bridgend Gardens and No.21 Castle Street - but we must visit them another day.

As we continue up the street passing Nos.23 and 25, listed as having an 18th century plastered facade to an earlier 17th century building, we come to what was once a tiny opening between 25 and 27, which led to "Sarah's Place".

Now, only the name remains, proof that once, six tiny cottages formed one of the many courts of Castle Street. Lack of imagination wiped away centuries of history.

No.27, known as St. Vincents, is again a 17th century timber-framed and plastered house, refaced at a later date in red brick, but retaining the original 17th century door. Once the Presbytery of the Roman Catholic Church, in 1851 it was the home of Godfrey Burdett, Attorney and Solicitor.

Nos.29 to 33 were once all one early 19th century timber-frame and plaster building. Now three cottages - evidence of the population explosion in Castle Street towards the end of the 19th century.

No.33 was the boyhood home of Mr. Cliff Stacey, local historian and former town clerk. It is now the home of Mr. and Mrs. Cecil Reed.

Mrs. Reed told me she has lived in Castle Street for 45 years, and her husband was a Castle Street boy, born in a cottage (now demolished) near to where the old Snowflake Laundry used to stand.

Round the corner from No.33 is Lower Square. Mercifully Lower Square has survived that holocaust known as Urban Planning and Improvement.

It was at No.2 Lower Square that I found 83 year-old Mrs. Dora Seaman.

Dora Seaman was born at No.17 Castle Street, one of four children. Her father, William Osborne, was a "horse-man".

'He loved horses, and every March when there was a horse sale on the Common, he would go to clip the horses' coats. He

155

made very good money, but unfortunately he loved his beer, and by the end of the day he was so drunk he didn't know how to get home.

'In those days times were hard and the beer was strong. Mother would often send us down to the Greyhound to tell Mr. Pledger not to serve father with any more drink!'

Like many people in Castle Street, Dora's mother traded at Mark Salmon's shop, and it was here that she would buy oil for her "Sunday lamp". This was a special oil lamp with a very pretty shade which was only lit on Sundays!

'No.7,' says Mrs. Seaman, 'was a sweet shop where we would buy our sherbet bags and "Tuffins". Tuffins looked like striped lollipops, but they were made of toffee and cost a halfpenny each.'

Little Dora Osborne went to the National School in Castle Street (now St. Mary's) and when she left, went straight into service as a "daily" to Mrs. Britton, wife of the butcher in Church Street.

During the First World War she left service to work at Engelmann's Nurseries, and afterwards went back into service as head house-maid to a wealthy American family.

But in 1926 Dora returned home to marry her childhood sweetheart, Fred Seaman.

Fred had been born at No.77 Castle Street, and for 27 years worked at Engelmann's Nurseries. Later, he became manager of the Co-op Coal Yard in Station Street.

No.2 Lower Square has been Dora's home now for over 56 years.

'In those early days we paid 4/9d (approx 25p) a week rent. The cottages belonged to the Roman Catholic Church and were always very well maintained.

'Of course at first there was no gas or electricity. But the Street was lit by gas lamps. Later, we changed from oil to gas, and then we thought we would like electricity, but we had to buy the electricity pole ourselves. It cost us £2.10s. (£2.50p).

'I'm afraid it *was* a rough street. The police had a very bad time. There used to be old P.C. Crickmore and another one called "Lightning" - that was because he was tall and very, very quick!

156

'Oh the fights on Saturday nights when they turned out of the pubs! Castle Street had a lot of pubs in those days.

'The men were very big and hefty. And they liked their food and their pint of beer. But they were really friendly people, and very good neighbours - always willing to help out.

'I have always been very, very happy here, and I still am!'

Returning once more to the main thoroughfare, we come to Walsingham House (No.35) the home of Mr. and Mrs. Nigel Weaver and their two daughters, Rachel 18 and Caroline 14.

The Weavers have lived in the town for 23 years, 11 spent at Walsingham House.

Nigel, a Health Services administrator in London, is an old-boy of the Friends' School, and admits that, during the time he was a boarder there, he thought Saffron Walden was 'the end of the earth'. Now he is older, he says he realises what a simply marvellous place it is.

The history of Walsingham House is an essential part of the town itself.

At the rear of the building, and an integral part of it, is the school house belonging to the old Grammar School.

The Grammar School is believed to be the oldest institution in the town, but little is known of its early history. The assumption is that it dates back to 1317 when, "Reginald, Scholemaster of Walden" is supposed to have been the first schoolmaster.

John Leche, Vicar of the Parish from 1489 to 1521 - one of the town's great benefactors - before he died requested his sister, Dame Bradbury, widow of Thomas Bradbury, Lord Mayor of London in 1509, to re-establish the school.

In 1522 Jane Bradbury obtained the necessary letters patent from the King. The licence was confirmed by Deed of 18th May 1525, which stated that the school curriculum was to be after the order of the Schools of Winchester and Eton.

William Dawson was the first master appointed by Dame Bradbury. But doubts arise as to whether the school house, which dates back to 1665, is the original one.

When James Burrows was appointed master in 1665, his first act was to restore and repair the school house.

Later, in 1817, the Corporation did the same thing and

157

uncovered a plaque with the date 1665 and the Latin inscription "Aut Disce Aut Doce Aut Discede" which roughly translated reads: "Either teach, learn or leave". (Believed to have been taken from the rules of the first Winchester School).

Originally the school house was free-standing. But, in 1825, the Master's house was built on the site of a cottage fronting the building, and a further extention which included an adjoining cottage was also incorporated in 1853.

The masters were poorly paid. The stipend of £12 never increased for many years. Consequently, the school suffered, until the arrival of the Rev. Alfred Enoch Fowler B.A., of Queens College Cambridge. Fowler was appointed master in 1846 and stayed until he retired in 1879.

There is an opinion that the Rev. Fowler moved the school to the grounds of his house at No.67 High Street.

Old rating lists state that the Rev. Fowler took up residence at No.67 in 1851, when the premises were referred to as "house and schoolhouse" but never again afterwards.

The rating lists of 1870 show No.69 High Street (next door) as "schoolhouse etc." (not to be confused with the Adult School which came later) and this continued until 1882.

The new Grammar School in Ashdon Road (now Dame Bradbury's) was built in 1881.

George Stacey Gibson donated £1,000 to the Building Fund, and also bequeathed a further £2,000 in his Will. As George Stacey Gibson owned both 67 and 69 until 1882, the idea that the Grammar School was carried on behind No.69 appears quite feasible.

The rating lists for Castle Street only go back to 1859, but No.35, although owned by the Grammar School Trustees, is recorded in this year as being "house and yard etc." rented by Charles Buck, never again referred to as "schoolhouse".

In 1876 William Pamphilon, carpenter, rented the property, succeeded by John Lucas Nash, later his widow, and later still, in 1933, one of his daughters and "T. Fall - Walden Pottery".

Thus it seems that the schoolhouse was used for almost a hundred years as some kind of small industrial premises.

Thankfully this delightful old building, now the Weavers'

dining room, was left more or less unspoiled - weather-boarded, timber-framed and plastered, with a peg-tile roof, and the original barrel-vaulted ceiling.

A row of 19th century desks, folded back against the wall, and a row of pegs on the wall opposite the door, remain evidence of the building's purpose.

Outside the walls are scored with the initials of many generations of boys, and even to this day, Iris Weaver is forever digging-up marbles in the garden!

With their heavily timbered and jettied gables Nos.37 and 39 stand either side of an entrance to a tiny courtyard. These, and the four cottages in the courtyard, are known as Bellingham's Buildings, and they brought a new wave of hope for some of the poorer families of Castle Street.

Historically and architecturally interesting, they represent splendid examples of late Victorian Domestic buildings, influenced by a growing trend which acknowledged the need for better housing for the working poor.

They were built in 1879 by the Trustees of the Amalgamated Societies (later to become the United Charities), on the site of the old Castle Street maltings.

The maltings, which belonged to the Gibsons and were rented by Joshua Clarke, eventually became the property of Lewis Fry, who sold them to the Trustees of the Amalgamated Societies for the sum of £300. Their demolition in the late 19th century again reflected the decline of the malting industry in the town.

The six dwellings on the site were named after James Gordon Bellingham, clerk to the Trustees, and represented the very latest in accommodation for the working-class.

At the time when most people shared outside privies and a cold water tap in the communal yard, Bellingham's Buildings provided untold luxury.

Each had its own outside lavatory, hot water from a tap heated by a kitchen range, and cold water from a tap over the kitchen sink. In addition there was a pantry and a cellar, as well as a good sized living room and three bedrooms upstairs.

But Bellingham's Buildings today, are no longer run by a charitable institution and are, for the most part, updated and privately owned.

No.4 is the home of Neil and Elizabeth Cameron and their two young children.

The Camerons, who come from Henley-on-Thames, first lived on the Fairview Housing Estate when they came to Saffron Walden a few years ago. But, as their family increased, they felt they would like an older-type property and consequently fell in love with No.4 Bellingham's Buildings.

'It is so convenient for town,' says Elizabeth, 'and Castle Street is a beautiful street. All the history of Saffron Walden is in this street.'

Continuing our walk along the northern side of the street, we pass Nos.41 and 43, described by the Department of Environment as follows:-

"An early 16th century timber-framed and plastered Hall House of the Wealdenhouse type, originally with a small hall between two bays. The bay at the west end has been demolished but one original corner post remains. The east bay has a jettied upper storey, and the front has continuous eaves, but the part which was originally the hall is set back slightly and has the original oak bressumer with curved brace supporting the eaves."

No.41 also displays some fine old cross-hatch pargetting - a much softer and more fluid form of decoration than its modern counterpart. Also, a lovely 19th century bay window.

This was probably the shop window of George Moss Taylor - Whitesmith - (one who makes domestic ironwork) who carried on his trade here from about 1869 until 1901.

The next group of cottages, Nos.45 to 51, according to Department of Environment records, again date from the early 16th century, altered during the 18th century, and form a continous range along with Nos.41 and 43.

Once more we see the changing fortunes of Castle Street mirrowed in this picturesque little row of houses. Large houses made into smaller houses, and these sub-divided to make tiny cottages, which later still are converted into larger houses again.

This makes the actual locating of certain premises extremely difficult and guesswork has to be relied upon I'm afraid.

Now we come to The Bell House, No.55, better known as The Five Bells.

Recorded as an early 17th century timber-frame and plaster building, altered in the 18th century or early 19th, this old beerhouse is now the home of Mr. Tony Skipper and his wife.

By a co-incidence, Tony is the Director of a Brewery company, and it was his work which brought them to this area six years ago. But, by that time, the Five Bells had long ceased to operate as a public house.

During the time they have lived in the town Sheila has taken an extremely active part in the running of The Home Farm Trust, as well as working part-time as a medical secretary at Saffron Walden General Hospital.

Tony, on the other hand, is gradually restoring the more interesting features of The Bell House in his spare time. Large open fireplaces have been opened-up and the fine old beams exposed, creating an atmosphere of great charm and gracious-ness not usually associated with old beerhouses!

Although The Bell House is not haunted, and Tony assured me that it is an extremly pleasant house to live in, he did refer to the story of the murder of Chief Constable William Campling.

Campling was shot in the legs as he left The Eight Bells in Bridge Street on the night of 31st October 1849, and later died of his wounds.

The story has it that the man who was charged with Campling's murder (but never convicted) was previously drinking in The Five Bells in Castle Street, and slipped out of the back door, across the fields and into The Eight Bells.

The Five Bells is believed to have been called The Waggon and Horses at one time. Apparently it was the custom for the Landlord to take his inn sign with him when he moved to another public house. This would account for the difficulty experienced in locating the sites of some of the other old pubs in the town.

The fields which William Campling's murderer crossed are now part of what we know as The Anglo-American Playing Fields.

These Playing Fields are a joint memorial to the officers and men of the 65th Fighter Wing of The United States Army Air Force, and the men and women of Saffron Walden who died in action or whilst serving their country during the Second World War.

161

The Americans stationed at Debden during the war inaugurated the scheme by raising £5,500, which in turn should have been matched by a similar sum raised by the town. This was in December 1947.

Unfortunately however, the funds raised by the town never actually met the required amount, and although the scheme was not abandoned, it was never really completed.

Nevertheless, the Memorial Playing Fields are a valuable amenity to the town.

Whilst we are here, it will be well worth a walk over towards the cricket pavilion, whose ornamental barge-boards proclaim its late Victorian origins.

This pavilion was first erected on the Common in 1871. In 1954 it was taken down and re-erected on its present site as part of the Memorial Playing Fields scheme.

Retracing our steps we walk through the imposing iron gates back into Castle Street, and pause to admire yet another range of old cottages.

No.57 to 63, recorded as 16th century timber-frame and plaster buildings, are believed to be actually much earlier in origin - at least in parts - and certainly in the case of No.61.

But perhaps the most interesting feature is the Scallop Shell on No.59 above the bressumer. This, together with the two ornamental brackets, are recorded as being 17th century.

The scallop shell is noted for being the emblem of St. James of Compostella. It was worn by medieval pilgrims who, on returning home after visiting the shrine of St. James at Santiago in Spain, usually placed a scallop shell in their hat to incite admiration.

The particular shape and size of the scallop shell on the front of No.59 tends to date from this period, so perhaps the man who first built this house, had made the pilgrimage. This would date the house much earlier than the 16th century.

The most intriguing house in Castle Street, is No.61. With its frieze of Chaucerian figures painted along the jettied upper storey, this delightfull cottage lends itself to much speculation and comment.

Mrs. Betty Hart who lives at No.61 told me that it used to be a barber's shop and then, later, an accountant's office.

'After we moved in people could not get used to the idea that

Mrs Hart at the door of No. 61 showing the famous frieze

it was a private house and would keep opening the front door and walking in!'

It was Mrs. Hart's daughter who hit upon the idea of painting the figures along the jetty - all characters from Chaucer's Canterbury Tales. Miraculously the idea worked! And people soon realised it was a private house.

When the house was repainted a few years ago, the frieze disappeared. Such was the outcry however, that Mrs. Hart's grand-daughter had to set to and paint in all the figures once more.

Mrs. Hart has lived in Castle Street all her life. First at No.59 when her parents started their married life living with her grandfather, Frank King, and now, many years later at No.61.

Many of the older generation will remember Mrs. Hart's grandfather, who died at the age of 94 in 1937.

Frank King was a builder and a stone-mason, and was one time general foreman for Bells who specialised in the restoration of old buildings and churches.

'In his youth he had worked on the Queen Mother's old home, and he used to tell us what a delightful little girl she was. He thought there was no-one else quite like her, and later, when she became Queen, he would always stand to attention whenever he heard the National Anthem played on the radio.'

Mrs. Hart's father (also Frank) followed in his father's footsteps, and it was he who, in August 1944, when helping Mr. Arthur Dix the builder, discovered the Dolphin on Dolphin House in Gold Street - a feature of the building which had lain hidden for many years beneath layers of plaster.

It was he who told her the story of the churchyard bones. Given the job of laying water in nearby St. Mary's churchyard, he and his men, whilst working, uncovered a mass grave full of old skeletons. Realising they had discovered a bit of local history, Mr. King went to find the Rector, which took rather a long time. When he returned to the site with the Rector they found all the bones had gone. His men had taken them to the pawn-shop and were at that very moment celebrating in the local pub. There was nothing else for it, the unfortunate Frank King had to put his hand in his pocket and redeem the missing bones.

Frank King junior was a great dancing man. He used to organise the dances at the Town Hall, and introduced the Charleston and the Tango to Saffron Walden, bringing down a couple from London especially to demonstrate it.

Mrs. Hart, who is now in her 60s, remembers the old days well.

'Oh yes, it was rough. The men would start fighting on Saturday nights when they came out of the pubs, and the women would finish it off on Monday morning in the Co-op.

'I once saw two women fighting under the counter in the Co-op.

'It was a street of pubs and chapels. Very mixed. You would get a tiny cottage – just two up and two down – and out would spill about 9 or 10 children, and you'd wonder where they put them all! And then, next door would be a fairly large house

Frank King junior with his dog Gyp

where they kept a cook and a maid. It was like that all the way along.

'I can remember the Misses Nash from Walsingham House. They were ladies of the old school - very genteel. Even though it was the 1920s and everyone was wearing short skirts, they would come along in their trailing Edwardian dresses and big wide hats. They never dressed any differently!

'But it was all great fun. There was never a dull moment, and really everyone got on very well together. They fought amongst themselves, but if anyone got into trouble they would all rally round.

'During the war the Germans bombed Debden, and a local man was killed. A few days later a German plane was shot down and two men bailed out with parachutes.

'Everyone in Castle Street rushed out with pitchforks and knives, and somebody got a wagon and they all piled in. Luckily for those Germans the American Military got to them before the Castle Street people did.

'On New Year's Eve everyone would join hands and dance round the church and in and out of all the pubs.

'And on Sunday mornings, a favourite sport with all the men was to take their dogs to catch rats.

'The local rat catcher would come along with a cage full of all the rats he'd caught during the week. He would stand by the lamp post (now removed) in the middle of the road (the junction of Castle Street and Museum Street) and let his rats out a few at a time, and the men would lay bets as to which dog would catch the most rats.'

Like most Castle Street children, little Betty King went to the National School – now St. Mary's – and she remembers how, on fine days, sometimes the teachers would allow them to take their lessons inside the old castle grounds.

When she left school, she went to work for Mr. Spurge the draper in King Street – now Booths – but after a fortnight she'd had enough. So she followed the other women in her family and went to work at the Snowflake Laundry.

The date on No.61 says "1411". And, judging from its massive, closely spaced timbers and enormous open-hearth fireplace, there can be no doubt that it is one of the oldest houses in the street.

Next door, No.63 is all part of the same building, and according to Mrs. Hart's grandfather, it was probably an old Inn at one time, part of which (No.63) was burned down and rebuilt at a slightly later date.

'My father bought Nos.61 and 63' says Mrs. Hart with a smile, 'from my grandfather in 1909. He paid £60 for No.61 and £30 for No.63. Times certainly change!'

But apart from the fact that No.61 is steeped in history and has watched the fortunes of Castle Street wax and wane, it is also filled with mementoes from bygone ages.

One of these takes pride of place on the wall. It is the bugle which sent the Saffron Walden Territorials on their way to war in 1914, and which blew the Last Post at the Cenotaph for those who did not return.

No.63 however, has its own history to relate.

In the middle of the 19th century it was a bakehouse belonging to Jabez Butcher. Later - at the turn of the century - a tiny greengrocer's shop owned by William Barker.

Behind No.63 is No.63A, a small industrial premises set so far back from the road that it could easily be missed.

Robert Tyer's Plumbing and Heating Contractors' business has operated on this site for over ten years and is an established part of the Saffron Walden industrial scene. But it was not without difficulty in the early days that Robert managed to set up his enterprise here.

When he first acquired the land in 1971, it was derelict and overgrown with trees and brambles. Naturally this had to be cleared to make way for offices and storehouses, and many local people objected.

Perhaps they were unaware that, for many decades, this site had been used for some or other small, industrial enterprise.

Rating lists for 1859 show a "house and butcher's shop" near this site. Later this was owned by John Willett (1865) and in 1873, "slaughterhouse, barn and stable" are recorded.

The slaughterhouse continued to operate until 1883, then appears to have fallen into dissuse. But from 1886 until 1887 or thereabouts, Thomas Hardwick the fishmonger rented the barn and stables.

Evidence of Thomas Hardwick's occupation was discovered by Mr. Tyer when excavating the floor of the barn to convert into a warehouse. Thousands of shells from every type of shellfish imaginable were found beneath the floor.

The stable was used for Hardwick's horses who, no doubt grazed in the pasture beyond. And possibly, another of the outbuildings was used as a smoke-house for smoking fish.

At a later date we find it described as "yard and buildings" owned by William Start, who in turn sold it to Frank King (Mrs. Hart's grandfather) to be used as a builder's yard.

Eventually, it became a storage depot for farm machinery belonging to the Start family of Little Walden. And Robert Tyer tells me that his smart, modern office was once, in fact, a pigstye!

Despite all the hassle, Robert's plumbing and heating business has successfully integrated itself into modern Castle Street.

Perhaps one of the reasons why the little backwater between Nos.63 and 65 became so overgrown and derelict was because yet another tiny community fell beneath the bureaucratic axe.

In 1937, the whole of Chapel Row was demolished under the rehousing scheme. Six tiny cottages housing families who had probably lived in them for generations, ceased to exist.

The actual location of these houses was behind Nos.65 to 69, and these three 17th century cottages are all that is now left of the tightly knit community which made up Chapel Row.

No doubt the people of Chapel Row were glad to leave, but with a little bit of foresight from the authorities Castle Street and Saffron Walden would have been historically much richer.

They call it "The City" but no-one seems to know why.

It starts at the junction of Castle Street and Museum Street, and includes the triangular piece of no-man's-land where the lamp post stood in the old days.

This is where the boys and girls of Castle Street gathered on summer evenings, and the men, with their dogs on Sunday mornings waited for the rat-catcher with his cage of rats.

It was here also that the old stocks stood for a while after they were removed from the market place in 1818. And it was

Junction of Castle Street and Museum Street

here probably that most of the dramas of Castle Street were acted or fought out.

Even a stranger senses there is something different about this upper part of the Street, hard to define yet unmistakably present.

Perhaps Miss Charlotte Berger and her friend Mrs. Harriet Webster felt it also when they came to preach to the sinners of Castle Street.

Charlotte Berger was born in Hackney in 1791, the daughter of wealthy parents. At the age of 21 she became a devout Christian and longed to spread the word of the Lord. But not until she met Harriet Webster did she seriously think of going out and preaching.

Mrs. Webster's parents had already established a number of Wesleyan Preaching Rooms between Ilford and Buntingford, and this gave the two young women the opportunity to travel from place to place spreading the word of the Gospel.

In 1820 they received a letter from a Mr. William Davies of Saffron Walden inviting them to preach in the town, and saying "there are many heathen here!"

A barn had been procured for the young women to preach in, and it is generally assumed that this was on the site of what is now the present Methodist Chapel in Castle Street. However there is another opinion which says that they hired a barn in the yard of the old Eight Bells in Hill Street (once the Pig Market, now Waitrose). And that it was not until two years later, after several visits to the town, that the ladies purchased a barn in Castle Street and converted it into a Chapel.

The young women, together with Mrs. Webster's parents, moved into a house nearby - Prospect House - set slightly back from the Street on the western side of the present Chapel.

What Chartlotte Berger thought of Castle Street in those days can best be summed-up by an entry in her journal, when she described her home as being "near to the courts of Satan".

There was strong opposition to the women preachers, and they suffered considerable harassment. The windows of their house were smashed; their garden vandalised; their water-butt drilled with holes and their services frequently inter-rupted by drunkards and hecklers.

But Charlotte Berger was not without courage, and lived on at Prospect House after the death of Mrs. Webster's parents, and Mrs. Webster herself in 1862. And she saw the realisation of her dream when the present Chapel was opened in 1865.

Since that time the Chapel has played an important role in the lives of the people of Castle Street. And, whilst the congregations of many churches throughout the country are fast declining, the congregation of Castle Street Methodist Chapel is steadily growing. Perhaps this is due, in no small way, to the present incumbent, The Rev. David Youngs and his wife Brenda.

David Youngs has been at Castle Street Chapel for five years. In the first place it was never his intention to become a Minister of Religion, he thought his vocation lay in medical research. But, like his wife, Brenda, he has been committed to the Methodist Religion from a very early age.

Prospect House once Miss Berger's home

Further, over the years he found he was becoming involved with youth work on an increasing scale. And, possibly it was his work with young people which prompted three different ministers - all family friends - within the space of six months, to ask David whether he had ever considered entering the Ministry. He says that after the third comment he felt it was more than just a co-incidence.

Entering the Church meant uprooting his family from their home in Royston and moving into Wesley House in Cambridge whilst he did his two years training. Fortunately he received whole-hearted support from Brenda, who is herself now training to become a local preacher.

Very much a family man, with four children (the eldest away nursing in London, the youngest asleep in her pram nearby) it is inevitable that most of David's family have become involved in some way with the activities of the Church.

But the highlight of the week for many young mothers in the area is undoubtedly the Thursday morning Mothers and Toddlers Group which is open to everyone of any denomination. This is run by Mrs. Daphne Cornell, who told me it was started just over a year ago with about half-a-dozen members. Now there are almost forty and the number is still growing.

Across the road from the Methodist Chapel stands a delightful range of 16th century timber-framed and plaster cottages - Nos.20 and 22. Known to many as "Reed's Corner" it was here that Thomas Reed set up his antique business in 1881, shortly after he was married.

Thomas Reed was a gamekeeper's son who went to work for a furniture manufacturer in London. He came home to marry an Ickleton girl, Mary Sewell, and started up his own antique business, first at No.19 High Street (now Coles the Bakers) and later, taking over the premises of Charles (Dick) Bird at No.20 Castle Street. And the Reeds have been in Castle Street ever since.

Thomas and Mary set up home next door to their shop and raised a family of three children, Frederick, Alfred George and Julia.

It was Alfred George, known simply as George, who entered the family business. Fred, the eldest, branched out on his own as a carpenter and undertaker at No.30.

Thomas Reed was a wellknown lay-preacher who would often be asked to preach in the outlying villages of Saffron Walden. But he always insisted on walking to his destination, saying, that his horse had worked hard all week pulling the cart piled high with furniture and the poor beast deserved one day of rest.

He had a purist's attitude towards antiques and would only stock seventeenth and eighteenth century furniture, occasionally making an exception in the case of very early nineteenth century pieces, but nothing as late as Victoria!

George Reed entered his father's business soon after

leaving school. When he married Ethel Harrington, a local girl, they came to live in the house next door to the shop, whilst Thomas and Mary moved to a house in Church Street (No.20) which is still owned by the Reeds and run as a secondhand furniture shop.

Like his father before him, George Reed preferred to stock only the best, knowing full well that there would always be a steady demand for high quality antiques. It is a criterion he handed down to his sons, Kenneth and Clifford, who now run the business.

The Reed family are so much a part of Castle Street, it would be impossible to imagine the Street without them. And although George's three daughters, Joyce, Margaret and Miriam, did not enter the family business, the fourth generation is now represented by Martin, Clifford's youngest son.

No.71 Castle Street faces the world with imposing 18th century dignity. In reality though, it dates from the 16th century, and like most buildings in Castle Street is basically timber-framed and plastered.

Now a private residence, it was, until quite recently, the Castle Inn, one of the many public houses in Castle Street. It was also the local dosshouse. Here, tinkers and tramps; the homeless and the jobless, could find food and shelter for a few pence a night in the outbuildings at the back of the Inn. And whatever short-comings the accommodation might possess, it was certainly a far better alternative to the Workhouse in Radwinter Road.

Next door to the Castle Inn stands Nos.73 and 75, all one 17th century timber-framed and plastered house, for many years known as "Charlie Farnham's Grocer's Shop".

Charles Farnham was a young man from Stapleford who came to sing at a concert in the Wesleyan Methodist Church in Castle Street, and fell in love with the young lady who was accompanying him on the piano - Julia Reed - the daughter of Thomas Reed the antique dealer. They were married in August 1911, and went to live in London, where Charles was manager of the International Stores in Portabello Road.

Living in London did not suit Julia, and when she became pregnant the doctor advised Charles to take his wife back to the country.

Meanwhile, Mrs. Harriet Reader who ran the General Stores next door to the Castle Inn, decided to move higher up the street. So, Thomas Reed purchased the Goodwill of the business for £60 for his daughter and son-in-law. (Remember most property was rented in those days).

Julia and Charles had three children, Maisie, Janet and David. Janet, who is now Mrs. Janet Tinnion, now lives in Gibson Close.

Talking about her childhood days in Castle Street between the wars (Janet was born in 1915) she says 'we were all very happy living in Castle Street. Later, when we moved to Church Street to keep my grandmother company, we were very sorry to have to leave.

'People used to say it was rough. But that was only in one or two places. When I think of our little area and some of the yards and courts, they weren't as bad as they were made out to be. They were all nice, warm-hearted people, and some of them kept their little homes very nice indeed.'

No. 73 about 1914 Charles and Julia Farnham and their daughter Maisie

174

'Of course we lived next door to The Castle Inn, and they used to have some funny customers there sometimes, because it was a Common Lodging House. But I was never afraid to walk around after dark. Perhaps there were fights, but probably they took place when I was in bed at night. I can't honestly say I remember any of them.

'I do remember "Monkey Start" who had a horse and cart, and every day stopped at the Castle Inn for a glass of beer, and always brought one out for his horse as well.

'And there was "Dealer Barker" who lived in Middle Square. He was an odd job man who worked on farms and anywhere he could find work.

'Then there was Blind Jim. He lived in Middle Square also. I suppose he lost his sight in the First World War. He was totally blind and never worked. I think he must have had a very sad life.

'And there was a Mrs. Woodley whom we always called "feathertoy" but I never did find out why.

'Most of my father's customers were very poor, and sometimes he had to wait quite a long time before he was paid. But he was known as a kindly man, and never minded waiting, because he knew they would pay in the long run.

'He had a motor-bike and side-car, and on alternate Sundays we were all packed in and we would go over to Stapleford to see his mother. As we got bigger it became too much of a squash, so he bought a secondhand car at an auction, run by Jennings in the Pig Market.'

When Thomas Reed died, the Farnham family moved into the house in Church Street where he and his wife had lived since the marriage of his son, George.

Maisie Farnham, the eldest of the Farnham children, married a local boy, Jack Taylor, in 1936, and eventually went to live near Norwich.

David, the youngest, volunteered for the airforce in 1939, became a pilot and was tragically killed in action at the age of 21.

Janet entered the offices of Woodward & Pridey, the auctioneers (now Watsons) after she left school. And, inheriting her parents' love of music, joined the Saffron Walden Operatic Society - thus sealing her fate!

It was at the Operatic Society she met Tom Tinnion, a young school teacher from Cumbria, recently arrived in Walden to teach at The Boys' British School in East Street. It was 1939, and they married just before D-day. Tom was now in the army, but it was through the kindness of his Commanding Officer that he managed to wangle special leave.

Tom is now retired from teaching and both he and Janet take an active interest in the life of the town. Janet, a keen golfer, was Captain of the Golf Club for 1969/70. She also continues her love of singing by singing in the Choir of The United Reformed Church.

At No.75 next door to Charlie Farnham's shop lived young Nellie Cornell with her children whilst her husband, also Charlie, was serving in the First World War.

Nellie, before she married, had been an Auger - another old Castle Street family who, for years had a confectioner's shop at No.38 (opposite the school). Charle had been a stoker at the Gas Works, and is still remembered by many as a one-time member of the Town Band.

Like the Farnhams, Nellie and Charlie had three children, Gladys, Marjorie and Charles. Unfortunately, both Gladys and Charles are now dead, but Marjorie – now Marjorie Sutton - lives in Mandeville Road.

Mrs. Sutton told me she was actually born in one of the little cottages in Church Path in 1911. But her parents moved soon afterwards to No.75 Castle Street where the Cornell's lived for many years.

Like many cottages in Castle Street at that time, No.75 was terribly damp. The owner of the property, who had a nice comfortable house in another part of the town, was, in all probability, completely indifferent to the plight of her unfortunate tenants.

Marjorie Sutton remembers a certain Christmas during the First World War when things were terribly scarce. Somehow her mother managed to obtain a Christmas tree, which she decorated on Christmas Eve with home-made sweets wrapped in brightly coloured paper. But, when they all came down on Christmas morning they found to their dismay that all the colours on the paper had run and all the sweets had melted in the incredibly damp atmosphere.

Charles and Ellen Cornell with Marjorie (left) baby Charlie and Gladys, 1917

177

The Cornells were very poor, but somehow Nellie always managed to make Christmas an occasion for her children. One Christmas she made her two little daughters rag dolls. But Marjorie was heartbroken when she discovered her mother's beautiful best blouse had been cut up to make dresses for the dolls.

But not all Mrs. Sutton's memories of Castle Street are sad. She remembers the pleasure she used to get from going upstairs in her Uncle Auger's shop and sorting out the bad oranges from the good.

'Oh the smell of those oranges! It took me right out of this world. I used to think of all the exciting, far away places they'd come from!'

One of her most vivid memories was the time they put straw on the road to deaden the horses hooves when the wife of the Landlord at the Five Bells was seriously ill.

Another is, of lying in bed and listening to the sweet, melodious voice of Molly Seaman, who sange like a nightingale as she walked back to her home in Castle Street late in the evening.

Young Marjorie went to Castle Street school.

'I loved school! Especially cookery. It was a great honour to be chosen to do cookery, only a few were allowed that privilege.'

After she left school Marjorie went to work for Mrs. Julius Green in King Street, and it was whilst working there a certain young man named Frank Sutton kept popping in on various excuses.

Frank worked across the road at Cleales Motor Engineers (now W.H. Smith's). He and Marjorie first met at a Scout Dance, and he was determined not to let grass grow under his feet, much to Mrs. Green's dismay. The latter could not understand why Marjorie should want to get married when she had such a good job! But she should have known that Marjorie was far too pretty to remain single!

No.24 Castle Street, together with Nos.20 and 22 originally formed all one 16th century timber-framed building.

For many years No.24 was the home of George Flack a carpenter who helped George Reed (Thomas' son) with the restoration of antiques. Later, when Fred Reed, the under taker and carpenter died at the age of 57, George Flack took over his business at No.30.

'The Flacks were a lovely couple,' says Mrs. Marjorie Sutton. 'Mrs Flack was a dressmaker, and it was she who made my dress for my grandad's funeral. In those days we always wore black at funerals' (1920s.)

Nos.26 to 34, dating from the late 17th or early 18th century were once two buildings, altered and sub-divided in the early 19th century.

Next we have Nos.36, 36A and 38, three picturesque pink-washed cottages recorded as being all one 17th century timber-framed and plaster house. Still remembered by many as yet another Castle Street pub - The Bell!

Sometime during the First World War, The Bell became the shop run by Mr. Alf Auger, brother of Nellie Cornell at No.75.

Alf Auger was also grandfather of young Fred Warner, who had been born next door at No.36 in 1922. Fred, who now lives in Huntingdon, remembering his boyhood in Castle Street, gave me the following account:-

'I attended the Infants School in Museum Street first, moving on to the National School which was situated virtually opposite my house.

'As I got older and progressed through the different forms, I well remember not troubling to get up in the mornings until 8.45am and having a quick wash so that I got to school just as the five to nine bell was ringing. This was always rung by the Head Boy on the instructions of the Headmaster.

'Mid-morning break was at 10.45. In summer my mother would come across with a large jug of lemonade and slabs of cake or buns. In winter we had steaming hot cocoa. All this went down very well with my mates – Arthur Butcher, Alf "Attie" Woodley, Joseph Elsom just to name a few.

'My grandfather and grandmother had a shop at No.38 and sold sweets, tobacco, vegetables, fruit and home-made ice-cream. Although his name was Alf Auger, he was commonly known as "Gruff", perhaps because of his manner.

'At that time there were very few vehicles about, so in summer we were able to play cricket in the street using the corner-stone of the Wesleyan Chapel as a wicket.

'We were nearly all boys from the National School,

Kenneth and Clifford Reed amongst them. Occasionally Middle Square would be used as a cricket pitch, but this was mostly reserved for football.

'I suppose Castle Street at that time was virtually two streets - the lower half stretching from Mark Salmon's Shop at the bottom and opposite Silletts' the bakers, right up to the The Five Bells public house - the top half consisting of The Castle Inn, Charlie Farnham's Grocer's shop, Bill Parish's fruit and vegetable stores, the Co-op and the Snowflake Laundry.

'There were several characters in the Street that I recall well - "Tiger Woodley, Monkey Start and Navvy Elsom" to name a few.

'On Saturday evenings in summer, we used to sit on Maberleys' wall, waiting to see if someone in the Victory had played the wrong domino and would consequently be asked to settle the argument at the bottom of Buckenhoe Barn Road.

'The Headmaster at the National School (now St. Mary's) was Mr. Robeson. He used to lie his cane across the front of his desk as a warning that he would not hesitate to use it, should it be necessary.

'I have fond memories of Mr. Hubert Doe, who I believe is still alive and living in the area, although I did not think much of him when he whacked me across the backside with Kenneth Reed's walking stick!

'My cousin "Tich Barker" lived opposite me and was, in my opinion, the best footballer the Bloods ever had. Although, lots of people said "Mop Whitehead" was the best player, but he was before my time.

'There are many more memories I could enlarge upon, but these I'm afraid are personal.

'One thing I would like to know is - who set fire to the paper in the school cellar? And - when the Fire Brigade arrived - who stuck nails in the waterhoses, causing the man holding the end of the hose to shout out - "there isn't much b.....water coming out of this end!" '

Fred Warner's father was, for many years, the manager of Isaac Marking's Butcher's shop on the corner of Church Street and Museum Street (now Weavers).

Fred married Margaret Smith, a local girl from Debden Road and ex-pupil of Cambridge House School.

They met whilst working at Emson Tanner's (now Rumseys and Gay Homes), he was the office boy and she, the office girl.

Now, after 43 years of marriage and three children, two daughters and a son in America, they are the proud grand-parents of four lovely grandchildren.

They left Walden in 1958 to live in Godmanchester, Huntingdon, where Fred runs his own Corn Merchants' business. But they still love to keep in touch with all their old friends in Saffron Walden, and try to visit the town whenever they possibly can.

The old school which played such an important part in the lives of Fred and the other Castle Street children has changed along with the times. Now known as St. Mary's Primary School, modernised and considerably enlarged, it is hard to associate it with the Victorian buildings of yesteryear.

No longer are the boys separated from the girls by a high wall. The old weather-boarded schoolhouse where the boys had their workshop and the girls their cookery lessons has long since gone. All that remains of this building is some linen-fold panelling in the Museum.

No-one seems to know the exact fate of the old cottage which once stood in the actual playground of the school.

Mr. Len Dix who helped pull the cottage down, says, it is believed to have been re-erected at Clavering, but of this he is not absolutely certain. The only evidence of this piece of Castle Street history is a small lead doll found under the floorboards of the cottage which is still in his possession.

Now, St. Mary's is very much a school of today with a computer, 22" colour T.V. and video. And no longer does the Headmaster - 38 year-old Mr. Mark Ferland - feel it necessary to sit with his cane across his desk.

In fact, he assured me that the Punishment Book which goes back to 1902 and is probably the original one, is used on very rare occasions.

'But I believe in discipline! Very much so! Thankfully we have very little trouble here. We like to treat the children in the same way that we would be treated ourselves.

'One thing I do insist on though - that is - sweets are just not allowed in school. This is for the sake of the children's teeth.'

He is full of praise for the children's parents who form an extremely active Parent Teachers' Association who work hard raising funds to augment the meagre educational allowances from the Authorities.

'With the drastic cuts in education though, it is extremely difficult to decide on priorities with the money raised by the parents. There is so much we need, and this year alone I must have spent £1,500 on books and microscopes and things.

'What does worry me, is the miserable state of the classrooms. The Authorities say there is no money for decorating classrooms, and some of them are in an appalling condition, they haven't been re-decorated for over 20 years.

'It is extremely depressing for both the children and the staff. Quite frankly, I am embarrassed when I show new parents around the school.'

Despite the peeling paint and plaster, there is undoubtedly a very happy atmosphere at St. Mary's. And the children no longer need to play cricket in the street, thanks to a willing staff who give up a lot of their spare time in extra-curricula activities.

And if mothers no longer greet their children with jugs of steaming hot cocoa at mid-morning break, the pupils have the advantage of a substantial mid-day meal at school, which is not averse to serving fish-fingers and beefburgers!

Sometimes a name, placed high up on a wall, reminds us that here lived yet another Castle Street community; under-housed, under-fed, under-priviliged.

But the people who struggled to survive in the tiny squares and courts like Hodson's Yard, Middle Square, School Row and Museum Court, left behind memories of a way of life that was hard - sometimes brutal - but which had an enviable richness money can never buy.

Mrs. Alice Jeffreys and her sister Mrs. Maggie Gypps were born almost at the end of the Castle Street era. Nevertheless they saw much of it, and were so much a part of it that they can still recall, with much laughter, what it was like in the "old days".

The old days for Alice and Maggie are the years immediately after the First World War.

Alice was born in 1916 and Maggie in 1918, in the "White Cottages" in Little Walden Road (near to the Golf Range). But at sometime in the early 20s they came to live at No.54 Castle Street - a large 18th century red brick house - once known as The Red Lion public house.

Their parents were Walter and Lily Elsom. No-one ever called Walter by his christian name though. He was "Navvy Elsom" to his dying day. No-one seems to know why although his daughters suggest it was because he was a big man and liked his beer!

Navvy Elsom and dog outside No. 54 in the 1920s

Deep down at heart Navvy was a coster. And like all true costers he had a fish, fruit and vegetable round with a horse and a cart gaily painted in true coster style by Mr. Dench, the sign-writer in Station Road.

He had little or no education, and although he could read, he could barely write, and often put a cross for his signature. He was however, a shrewd businessman and knew how to count, and his capacity for mental arithmetic would put a pocket calculator to shame.

Navvy's business prospered, and when his son Bert ("Dink") joined him he was able to have two horses and carts on the road.

As time passed by the horses and carts were replaced by vans, still painted with the old coster whirlygigs and his motto "live and let live" on the doors at the back.

Sometimes, at the end of the day there would be quite a lot of white fish left, and because in the 20s there were no refrigerators, the fish would be "put through the pan" and sold next day as cold, fried fish.

The next thing Navvy and Lily did, was perhaps inevitable, they opened what was to become the most important institution in Castle Street, second only to the pubs (the chapels came third) - a fish and chip shop.

Elsoms' fish and chips were, by everybody's standards, considered the best in Walden, and people would travel for miles to buy their "bit and a pen'orth". (Fish was 2d., chips 1d.)

Naturally the bulk of the work fell onto Lily's shoulders, although the children were made to pull their weight. Alice and Lily, who went to the National School opposite, say it didn't matter how late they were at dinner-time, they always had to wash-up before going back to school.

Lily cooked her fish and chips in three huge pans heated by coal fires underneath. (Gas followed much later). The chips themselves were made by putting the potatoes through a chipping machine by hand. 'And goodness knows how many chips you got for a penny in those days!' laughs Maggie.

Then there were the fritters. The people living in the tiny courts and squares off Castle Street were just not poor - they were absolutely destitute. The little children would come into the shop to watch Lily frying the fish, straining off the crispy bits of batter from the boiling fat and putting them to one side. Their eyes would be round with hunger, longing and anticipation.

Lily, knowing full well they hadn't a penny to their name, would look down at them and say "do you want some fritters then dear?" and would place a large helping of crispy bits of batter into a piece of paper for each child.

Meanwhile Alice and Maggie were growing up. They comprised the younger element in the family, envied by their four elder brothers and their sister Nell, who felt that Alice, Maggie and baby brother Joe "had it a bit too cushy".

Not that Navvy and Lily ever did over-indulge any of their children. In the early days in Castle Street when Navvy was struggling to get on his feet, the Elsom's were poor, like most of their neighbours. But they never went hungry, and Lily kept all her family immaculately clean.

Boots had to be polished every night for school next day, and Sunday clothes kept strictly for Sunday and special occasions only.

'We wore boots for school,' say Alice and Maggie, 'and on Sundays what we called "low ankles" (lace-up shoes which just reached to the ankles). And you dare not wear your low ankles for school on peril of your life!

'We all had our special jobs. But on Sundays we were expected to go to the Primitive Methodist Chapel at the top of the Street, three times. If we didn't, George Reed, who was the Sunday School Superintendent, would tell our Dad, and we wouldn't get our "wages".

'When we came home from Sunday School on Sunday afternoon, Dad would be sitting at the table and he would dole out our weekly penny pocket money, which we called our wages.

'Then we would fly down to Alf Auger's, who was always open on a Sunday for a "ha'porth of mixed". He would bring out a big 7lb tin of all sorts of mixed toffee, and put a handful in the middle of a square of newspaper from a pile kept ready cut for the purpose. He never weighed the toffee.

'By the middle of the week we'd spent all our wages, so we would look round for empty bottles. You could always get a penny back on an empty bottle.'

Both girls left school at fourteen. Alice first, to stay at home to help Lily in the house and in the shop.

When Maggie left she went "straight on the rounds", helping her father and brother, Dink, until young Joe left school two years later.

Joe, like Dink, became an integral part of the business, and continued working in the family firm until he retired ten years ago.

Each of the girls married at the age of 18. Alice married Bob Jeffreys whose father, a retired Metropolitan Police Sergeant kept the White Hart at Wimbish. Like Maggie, she met her husband "round the Mansion."

'In those days there was nowhere to go and nothing to do, so, on Sunday evenings the thing was, to get all dressed-up and walk round the Mansion (Audley End). It didn't matter whether it was light or dark, everyone would be there.

'All the country boys from the surrounding villages would be there, sometimes with their bikes. And you'd be surprised how many people met their husbands that way!'

Despite the fact that Alice and Maggie say "there was nowhere to go and nothing to do" they certainly seem to have managed to enjoy themselves.

Highlight of their week was the sixpenny hops on Saturday nights held at the various village halls. The girls would rush round on Saturday to see if they could muster up a party of 12 or 14 so that they could hire a taxi.

'You could get 'em all in a six-seater with a push!

'When you got there, you'd go to the pub first. You'd only have to buy your first drink, because there was always somebody willing to buy you a second.

'After you'd had a couple of drinks, you'd be ready for the dance. And because we were the lively ones, we would get all the partners, whilst the other girls would be sitting round the walls with long faces.

'Dad used to get hopping mad when we were getting ready for the Sixpenny Hop. We were the first in the Street to have electricity and thought we were very posh. But, if he saw that we had the light on in our bedroom whilst we were getting ready, he'd shout up - "put that ......light out!" We were always expected to use candles in the bedrooms.'

Tragedy struck the Elsom family when Lily died at the age of 54 in 1937. Navvy never really recovered from her death, and Alice, by this time married, came back to Castle Street with her husband to live at No.54.

So Bob Jeffreys entered the Elsom family business, and with the passing years the name Jeffreys superseded the name Elsom. Alice was left a widow at the age of 38, but still continued working in the shop, and with the concerted efforts of other members of the family the fish and fruit round continued.

Now, her two sons, Robert and Roy, carry on the tradition that their grandfather laid down almost a hundred years ago. Their vans cover a ten mile radius surrounding Saffron Walden, and they never need to advertise, the name Jeffreys speaks for itself.

When I asked Alice and Maggie why they called this part of the Street the City, they laughed.

'Perhaps it was because there was more life at this end of the Street! There were so many yards and courts around. And goodness knows how many children there were in those two-up two-down cottages with one tap in the yard where everybody got their water, and a row of lavatories - two cottages to one lavatory.

'But everyone seemed to be happy. We were never bored. There was always somebody to talk to in the Street. On summer evenings those who lived at the bottom of the yard (Museum Court) would come up to the top, and lean on a bit of old wooden fence which surrounded the garden of the first cottage.

'In the middle of the road all the children would be playing. There wasn't any fear of cars coming up the street.

'And of course the shop would be open late at night. When they came out of the pub, they all wanted fish and chips. And Dad would sit outside talking to his customers with his dog by his side.

'As children we had the road to ourselves. We had different games for different times of the year. First it was skipping, then hopscotch, next knocking down tilers, then marbles and in the autumn, conkers of course.

'We never found the street rough. People would speak their

minds, but they were honest, and they wouldn't owe you a penny. They called it "the ready money" Street!'

Maggie Elsom married Frank Gypps who also entered the family firm after serving in the Second World War, and who managed the Thaxted Branch of the business.

Although for a number of years Maggie and her husband lived away from Castle Street, 15 years ago they bought No.81, one of the three Victorian red-brick villas almost opposite the old family home. When asked what brought her back to Castle Street, she replied simply 'Castle Street'.

Every child who went to the National School at one time knew No.50 Castle Street simply as "Parrish's". The place where, with much thought and deliberation, an old-fashioned penny could be wisely invested in a bag of toffee big enough to last all day. A momentous decision for any schoolchild and one not to be rushed.

Today, this delightful 17th century timber-framed building is no longer the school tuck-shop. Once two tiny cottages, and now all one house, it brings its own unique charm to this particular part of the Street.

It stands at the corner of a small opening which once led to Museum Court – one of those tiny, teeming communities which disappeared shortly after the Second World War, housing colourful characters of Castle Street.

Men like Catty Start who lived next door to the Parrish's and Dobbie Richardson. The latter, known as "Sixer" because, one night, after a drinking bout, it took six policemen to hold him down.

Then there was Middle Square - Stennetts Yard - in the early 19th century. And, on the other side of the school - School Row - another microcosm of struggling existence.

It was here that young Rosetta (Polly) Johnson lived for a short while after she married. Polly, whose maiden name was Woodley, worked at the Skin Factory in Upper Square. And every evening a young shepherd from Westley Farm in Little Walden Road, waited outside the factory to walk Polly back home to Littlebury. His name was Jim Rushworth, and they were married in 1916.

Polly and Jim left School Row to live at No.56 Castle Street

Polly Johnson used to live at No. 56

with Jim's widowed father. There Polly remained until she was moved to No.6 Catons Lane under the rehousing scheme of the 1940's.

Polly did not regret leaving Castle Street, and says, 'I always vowed that once I got out of that street I would never go back!'

This, despite the fact that, in her own words 'there weren't better neighbours goin'! 'We were poor - but I'm telling you not a word of a lie - there weren't better neighbours goin'.

There are those of us who regret the demolition of historically and architecturally interesting buildings. But, to those who lived in these tiny cottages, the new council houses in Little Walden Road, Catons Lane and Thaxted Road, represented hope, and a better chance in life.

Mrs. Marjorie Sutton, at that time living in Museum Street with her parents, says, 'I remember, there was such a fight as to who would get Council Houses. Everyone wanted a Council House!'

'The deciding fact was,' says Mrs. Dora Seaman of Lower Square, 'whether you had a mixed family. We only had one daughter, so we stayed. Those with boys and girls were given the opportunity of a Council House.'

Seven out of the ten children born to Polly survived. And Jim died when he was still in his thirties.

But Polly never lacked for good friends when she needed them most.

She recalls during Jim's last illness, how Navvy Elsom brought back two small bottles of Guiness and put them inside her front door for Jim, every time he went up to The Victory. And how, on Sunday mornings, he would bring round a tray of fish to help Polly feed her hungry brood.

Mrs. Cornell, her neighbour at No.58, would come in each day to sponge down the sick man. And Mrs. Adams, the proprietoress of the Snowflake Laundry, never let a week go by without sending her daughter across with a large basket of fruit.

'I knew nearly everyone in the Street,' says Polly, 'and if they didn't see you out for a few days, they would come and knock on your door and ask if you were alright.

'Yes, the fighting was terrible. They were always fighting. I have never seen anything like it. They would throw one another on the floor, then jump on them and nearly trample them to death.

'There was one family in particular, and I bet you a shillin' if they'd been out on the beer, there would be a fight in the yard! Their sister Suke would come out with the poker and say - I'll hit you across the ....head - but poor old Suke would always get the worst of it!

'We had some good times though. There was poor old Dobbie Richardson, who used to go up and down the Street when he'd had a glass of beer, singing like a nightingale until long past midnight.

'For a short while he lodged along of me. He was a good old boy mind you! But when he'd had a drop of beer, he would not come in. And my husband used to go out and get hold of his arms, but he still wouldn't come in. So I used to go out and say - well ....you - stop out all night!

'P.C. Clap-clop soon settled them all down though. Everyone was scared stiff of him.'

Before Polly left Castle Street she married a second time. Alec Johnson was a builder's labourer who actually worked on the house in which she lives now.

Alec died early on in life, and once again Polly's wonderful neighbours rallied round. But she tells a strange tale of a night just before Alec died.

Polly's brother Bob came over each evening from Littlebury to sit with the dying man for a while. On this particular evening, they both knew that Alec was very near to his end, so Bob said he would stay the night to keep Polly company.

During the course of the evening Bob got up to go to the outside lavatory. But, within seconds he was back in the living room with a face as white as paper.

'Do you know you've got something in your yard all in white?' he said.

'No Bob,' she replied, 'there's nothing in the yard!'

However, for a long time the frightened man would not "go across the yard" until in the end he simply had to! On his return, he swore to Polly that an apparition all in white was waiting for him when he came out of the lavatory. It never spoke, just hovered in the air. Two days later Alec was dead.

In the Almanack for 1886 we find John Kettle the Rag Merchant living at No.56, to be succeeded by Stephen Reed.

Stephen Reed, advertising himself as "Marine Store Dealer" in the 1904 Almanack says - Special Prices quoted for quantities of Metal, Brass, Copper, Lead, Zinc etc. Dealer in Rags, Iron, Horse Hair, Rabbit and Mole Skins in any quantities.

Undoubtedly he would have been an essential part of the life of Castle Street, and many a poacher must have knocked on Stephen Reed's door late at night.

Now Polly's old home is the home of Mr. And Mrs. Geoffrey Rolf and their two little daughters, Caroline eight and Julia six.

The Rolf's have lived at No.56 for ten years, and have

gradually restored it to its original compact Regency charm.

Geoffrey is a British Telecom Manager, and Diana a professional librarian working on a voluntary basis in the Town Library.

Diana showed me the old yard with the "haunted?" privy, Polly's old wash-house and the brick and flint wall dated 1813.

Next door and beyond - numbers 58, 60 and 64 were originally four 18th century timber-framed cottages. And in 1851 No.58 was a Greengrocer's shop owned by Ruth Hodson.

Fifty years ago, No.64 was the home of Hubert Clarke, a young lorry driver who won the heart of a certain Miss Florrie Banks, a young lady from Wimbish.

Florrie, like many girls of her generation went into service as soon as she left school, and at the age of 15 came to Saffron Walden to work for Dr. Mahon the Church Organist.

It was her Aunt who told Florrie's father that she had seen 'your Florrie out with someone from Castle Street!'

It was a statement enough to strike terror in the heart of any self-respecting local parent in those days! Especially if they themselves were unfamiliar with the Street and its people.

True love eventually won through, and Florrie and Hubert were married in Wimbish Church on the 29th February 1936, notwithstanding the fact that the Vicar had said he never performed weddings in Leap Year!

The young couple set up home at No.70 Castle Street, a few doors along from Hubert's parents, and despite the early misgivings of Florrie's parents, it was an extremely successful marriage.

Hubert died in 1974, just before his first grandson was born in Utah, U.S.A.

Strangely enough, history repeated itself when their daughter Janet married an American because Hubert could not stand Americans!

'I think it was because so many American Servicemen used to hang about Castle Street during the war,' says Florrie.

But like his own marriage, everything worked out very well, and Hubert's fears proved to be completely unfounded.

Fortunately Beryl, their eldest daughter, married someone

a little closer to home and is now within easy reach in Bury St. Edmund's.

Mrs. Clarke says she has always been extremely happy living in Castle Street. Although when she and Hubert first moved into their house, it was far from being as comfortable as it is now. Because of course, even in 1936 there were few mod cons in Castle Street.

'It was all extremely hard work - especially on washing days. All the washing was done in the big, old-fashioned copper in the kitchen - filled - jug at a time - from the communal tap in the yard behind the house. Which, surprisingly enough, never seemed to freeze up during cold weather.

'I didn't even have a mangle in the early days of our marriage, and sometimes it would take all week for the clothes to dry when the weather was wet.

'I used flat irons to iron the clothes, and there was always one standing on the back of the kitchener, warm and waiting, should anything need to be ironed in a hurry.

'We bathed in a big tin bath in front of the old kitchener with its big steel fender. Oh how I remember that steel fender! I must have rubbed my fingers to the bone polishing it with emery paper!

'We lived mostly in the kitchen because we couldn't afford to keep two fires going. But at Christmas and sometimes at the weekend we would light a fire in the front room.

'The yard was lit by a gas-lamp on the wall, and the lavatories were right up at the other end of the yard, two cottages to one lavatory. It wasn't very pleasant on a cold winter's night if you wanted to spend a penny.'

But Florrie has no regrets. Hubert proved to be a good, hardworking husband with a steady job driving for Hasler's the corn merchants. And eventually the Clarke's were able to buy their cottage and make it their very own home.

'Yes,' she admits, 'there were some rum characters in the street in the old days. They were nearly all Barkers or Starts! All of them huge people. They could pick up a heavy sack as if it was a pound of sugar! They had to be strong of course - because most of them did such heavy work.

'I remember Monkey Start, he always had Geraniums in his

window, and he had a large Dalmatian dog. During the blackout (Second World War) he always boarded up his window, but one night for some reason he just couldn't get the board up - so - swearing like a trouper he left the window uncovered. But he was a nice, kindly old man really.

'Then, there was the story of the woman who pushed her husband up the chimney because she didn't want him to go into the army.

'Across the way there was a little shop (now Nos.107 and 107A) kept by a Mrs. Harriet Reader. She was a quaint old lady who went to the Primitive Methodist Chapel every Sunday morning dressed in an old-fashioned bonnet and cape.

'And then there was the Co-op! It was a lovely old place, and Reg Bassett the manager was a great character.'

But Mrs. Clarke, a youthful 76 year-old, does not spend all her time living in the past. She visits her daughters whenever possible, as well as taking a keen interest in the life of the town and being an enthusiastic member of The Towns Women's Guild.

The yard at the back of Mrs. Clarke's home is called Castle Court. If you did not know it was there, you might easily think it never existed. Or perhaps, like so many Castle Street yards, gone for all time, perpetuated in the name high up on the wall.

Florrie Clarke remembers it as a collection of 'funny little cottages, one up and one down and a cellar beneath.'

Thankfully the cottages still stand, now modernised and improved.

No.4 Castle Court is the home of Mr. and Mrs. Tony Bates and their two children, Lynn 17 and Paul 14. Tony, a builder, came to Castle Street with his parents when they took over the Castle Inn for a number of years.

Forty-seven year-old Barbara Bates is a Castle Street girl. She was born in Middle Square and remembers the Street as it was, just before the massive post-war rehousing scheme.

'None of the houses backing on to the meadow in Middle Square had back doors. As children we used to have a ladder propped against the window so that we could climb down to play in the meadow' (now part of the school playing fields).

'But I liked the street as it was. Everybody said it was

Castle Court

rough. But it wasn't - not in my personal time! It always seemed to have such a happy atmosphere, and everyone was so friendly.'

Like Middle Square, Camps Yard was also part of the rehousing scheme for this part of Castle Street, and so it too has disappeared. In its place are smart new houses, and No.91, the home of Mr. and Mrs. John Carter, is one of these.

John Carter is a Walden man, who lived at Bridge House when he was a boy, but moved to London soon after he left school. After an absence of 50 years John felt he would like to return to his home town, so he and his wife Margaret, bought No.91 Castle Street 14 years ago.

To be strictly accurate, No.91 and its neightbour 93, stand on the site of what was once the Snowflake Laundry.

The Laundry building had previously been the head-quarters of The Salvation Army, which in turn had previously been The Black Horse - another of Castle Street's notorious beerhouses.

William Barker, who had a greengrocer's shop at No.63 Castle Street in the first decade of this century, was a prominent member of The Salvation Army, which in time earned him the nickname of "Soldier Barker".

Charles Adams and his wife Sylvia opened the Snowflake Laundry in 1907. For many years Charles Adams had been running a grocery and haberdashery store next door to the Salvation Army, which was eventually to become the first Co-op shop in Walden.

For it was in Castle Street that the Saffron Walden District Co-operative Society was born.

Against fierce opposition from local traders, the Society was registered on March 1st, 1902, starting in the taproom of The Bell public house (Nos.36-38). And from that day onwards a bell has been used as the Society's seal for all important transactions.

Shortly after opening at The Bell, the Co-op moved across the road to No.99, where it stayed until 1951, when a purpose

Snowflake Laundry Van

built shop was opened on a site on the other side of the Laundry. And until its quite recent demise, this little shop has always held a special place in the hearts of the people of Castle Street.

As did Charles and Sylvia Adams. Not only did they run the Snowflake Laundry for over 60 years, employing many of the women of Castle Street, but they were themselves, kindly caring people.

The weekly basket of fruit to Polly Johnson with her dying husband and hungry brood of children, was just one of the many kindnesses they performed.

And Marjorie Sutton remembers how, as a child during the First World War, when the German Zeppelins came over, Mrs. Adams allowed the terrified people of Castle Street to shelter in the Laundry. When the raid was over, it was she who handed out steaming hot cups of tea to everyone.

'I used to love going into the Laundry,' says Mrs. Sutton. 'One of my most exciting memories is of the large quantities of beautiful brown paper on the counter. I'd never seen such lovely brown paper in all my life. So crisp and fresh-looking, ready and waiting to wrap the clean laundry.'

Sylvia Adams continued with the Laundry after the death of her husband. And when she died, Marian, one of her two daughters, and her son Albert, carried on the business.

Unfortunately, Marian, brought up to be staunch Church of England, disgraced herself by marrying a Methodist Minister!

However, Albert carried on until he finally retired in 1968, when the business was taken over by the Saffron Walden Laundry Company in Gold Street.

Mrs. Betty Hart worked at the Snowflake Laundry for many years and says, 'the machinery was really very old. One of the washing machines dated back to 1864 and it was worked by steam - but it certainly worked and the washing was beautiful!

'Because most of the machinery was so old and falling to bits, a great deal of the ironing was done by hand. But the women were marvellous ironers. And you should have seen the enormous irons they used.

'Everything was done to perfection. All the tablecloths and

197

the serviettes were measured first to ensure they came out exactly the right size when they were finished.'

Although the Laundry was removed to another part of the town, working under another name, it was the end of an era for Castle Street when the doors finally closed for the last time.

By the end of the 1960s the old, colourful personalities of Castle Street were fast disappearing. Even old "Clap-clop" the policeman whom everyone feared, had finally retired.

'He was a smashing chap really,' says one anonymous admirer. 'But he was a policeman all the time - never off duty! He'd see you in the Market Place in the morning and tell you a joke, and nick you at the end of King Street in the afternoon! He was fine as long as you didn't break the rules, but if you did - heaven help you!'

Not every change in Castle Street has been for the worse however. And the "Lollipop Lady", Mrs. Betty Shepherd, is one of the more pleasing innovations which have arisen from the increase in traffic in the Street.

Mrs. Shepherd, who lives in Castle Cross, has been the Castle Street Lollipop Lady since April 1984, but is certainly not new to the job. She says she was a school crossing attendant about 14 years ago. When a vacancy occurred in Castle Street a few months ago, so many mothers approached her and begged her to apply for the job that she decided she would, because she knew just how dangerous the Castle Street crossing is.

She says she loves doing it. 'The only time I don't like it is, when it is wet and miserable. But I feel I am performing a very useful service, and I know that all the children will get to school safely if I am here. After all, I have been a young mother myself, and now I have young grandchildren.'

But perhaps nowhere in Castle Street is the 20th century more architecturally obvious than at the top end, on the northern side, where modern houses have replaced many of the old cottages and landmarks.

No.109, an early 19th century brick house, now painted a neat black and white is the sole survivor of decades of change at this end of the street. Here, in 1904, Arthur Marsh had his Baker's shop. Advertising in the Almanack for that year he

198

says, "Bakings carefully attended to. Families waited upon daily. A trial respectfully solicited."

A quick glance at the old rating lists shows that No.109 had been a "Baking Office" since 1869 at least, and probably much earlier than that. But now, like so many other once-flourishing Castle Street businesses, it has become a private residence.

This house officially brings us to the end of Castle Street - a long street, whose history has left an indelible mark on the history of the town.

But high on Castle Hill, adjacent to the Castle itself, stands the old Primitive Methodists' Chapel.

The exterior of the building has changed little since it was first built in 1836. But since the amalgamation of the Primitive Methodists with the Wesleyan Methodists in 1939, the Chapel has enjoyed a strangely chequered existence.

So many of the old Castle Street families belonged to the Primitive Methodists. The Farnhams, the Elsoms, and of course, the Reeds.

George Reed the Antique Dealer was the Sunday School Superintendent, and kept a watchful eye on the younger

Mrs Julia Farnham, Mrs Claire Holland, Alice Reed, Minister's wife Mrs Sellers and Jean Reed

members of the congregation. His brother Fred played the organ, whilst the younger members of the family, Kenneth, Clifford, Margaret, Julia, Winifred and Jean, all helped to swell the congregation.

But what do you do with an old Chapel when the congregation moves lower down the Street? Well, you can turn it into an ice-cream parlour for one thing.

"The Castle Creamery" will be remembered by many people who were children at the time when Mr. Murphy, the owner, had his ice-cream round, and gave what he didn't sell to the children around about.

In 1958 the Castle Creamery was bought by Sidney Bailey, an enterprising young engineer who, having spent his earlier working years in the packaging industry, decided to venture out on his own. So the Chapel then became "The Castle Printing Works." The Castle Printing Works proved to be the birthplace of one of the town's major industries - UTP Packaging.

From humble beginnings, using converted machinery to print cellulose film for confectionery, UTP Packaging now leads the country in food packaging.

In 1960 The Castle Printing Works moved to Shire Hill Industrial Estate, changing its name along with its new address. And, at the same time, the Chapel became the headquarters of John Brown Ltd, a building company with a high reputation for the quality and design of their houses.

The Company consists of Mr. John Brown himself, his wife Betty - who is the Secretary of the Company - and Colin their son, recently made a Director; office manager Bob Barber, assistant office manager Chris Charlton and "Frani" Saich, site manager, and a workforce of 25 highly qualified men who have never been laid-off for lack of work!

Even to an outsider, it is obvious that John Brown Ltd. is a family firm in more than one sense of the word. And it is not surprising to learn that fifty per cent of the staff have been with the Company since it was first formed 18 years ago.

On the eastern side of Castle Hill stands Castle Hill House, now called "The Beeches." A fine house of generous proportions and 18th century splendour. Once the home of "The Maberlys" it is now converted into four self-contained flats.

Its gardens and orchards given over to another imposing complex of modern town houses known as "Maberly Court".

If, in the old days, every village had its "Big House" and its "Squire" then Castle Street, a community as closely knit as any village, had "Maberlys" with Gerald Maberly, Barrister at Law, as the Squire.

The Maberlys lived at Castle Hill House for the greater part of this century. Gerald Maberly was a prominent member of the Literary and Scientific Institute; an enthusiastic supporter of the Bacon Theory on the authorship of Shakespeare's plays, and a staunch Liberal.

Every year, the huge iron gates of Castle Hill House were thrown open for the annual Liberal Fête, which was held in the grounds.

These gates, with their twin laburnum trees on either side - cascades of golden blossom in early summer - were a wellknown feature of Maberlys. Now - like so many other well-loved and familiar features - they are just another memory.

At Christmas time, Gerald Maberly would present prizes to those children of the National School in Castle Street who had come top of their classes in exams.

Nothing lasts forever. The Maberlys are gone, and the children of St. Mary's School no longer sit on the wall on Saturday evenings in summer, waiting - like young Fred Warner and his chums - for someone to make a hurried exit from The Victory across the way.

Finally we come to the Castle. A grim, grey ruin of a fortress which gives its name to both hill and street.

It was built by Geoffrey de Mandeville in the 12th century and is a massive construction of flint rubble and extremely hard cement, with walls 12 feet thick and 25 feet high (believed to have been much higher at one time).

It is said that it occupied 20 acres originally, and what we see today are just the foundations and dungeons of the Keep. And at the beginning of the century the old pillory from the prison house at Newport and the stocks - after they were removed from the Castle Street/Museum Street corner, were kept here.

The start of Museum Street

CHAPTER EIGHT

Museum Street

First published in the Saffron Walden Weekly News
February 14 March 3rd – 1985

Originally Museum Street was called "Pudding Lane" – no-one seems to know why – but by the 18th century it had become "Little Church Street". Frank Emson in his "History of Saffron Walden" says this was because it joined Church Street and Castle Street and passed close by the east end of the Church.

But it is generally assumed that the name was changed when the Museum opened in 1835.

It forms part of a Medieval crossroads, believed to be unique, in that they have remained unchanged throughout the history of the town.

On the corner of each road stands a medieval house, and on the north-west corner – officially known as 24 Church Street, – is "Weavers" – an exclusive china shop coupled with one of those delightful old-world tea-rooms so difficult to find these days.

The owner, Mrs. Bretten, who admits she is completely new to this sort of thing, started business almost a year ago.

As the premises had previously been both a butcher's shop and a freezer centre, extensive alterations were necessary. And it was whilst these alterations were in progress that evidence was found to support the theory that No.24 was actually two buildings dating from medieval times.

I asked Mrs. Bretten why she called her shop Weavers. She said that after a lot of research she couldn't find a suitable name connected with the shop so, she decided on Weavers because of the weaving industry carried on extensively in Saffron Walden at one time.

But for many people Weavers will be remembered always as "Isaac Marking's Butcher's Shop".

Isaac Marking took over what must be assumed was a family business in 1879. John Player, described by Henry Hart in his memoirs, as "Butcher of Gold Street and High Street", appears to have bought No.24 in 1824 according to the rating lists.

John Player died about 1847 and the business was continued by John Nash on behalf of Elizabeth Player until Isaac Marking took over.

According to Sir Henry Marking, son of the late Isaac Marking junior, the Players, Nashes and Markings were all inter-related. And Sir Henry himself has in his possession a butcher's steel bearing the inscription "I.P. 1777" inlaid in silver on the ivory handle.

(As a matter of interest, the Players of Players' cigarettes are a branch of this family also).

Isaac Marking junior, the "son" in Isaac Marking & Son, took over the business in the first decade of this century according to records.

After his death in the 1940s., his manager, Herbert Warner, ran the business for Mrs. Hilda Marking until it was sold in the 1950s and continued as manager until his own sudden death in the 1960s.

Herbert Warner was born in Stansted, and served in the Coldstream Guards during the First World War. After he was demobilised he came to Saffron Walden to work for Isaac Marking.

Getting off the train in Station Road, he asked the first person he met, a coal-man by the name of Charlie Luckings, if he knew where he could find lodgings.

Charlie Luckings was related to Gruff Auger, and so he directed Herbert to No.36 Castle Street, and thereby sealed Herbert's fate. A few years later young Herbert married Gruff Auger's only daughter.

Isaac Marking junior and his wife Hilda were both deeply involved with the life of the town.

Hilda's maiden name was Street, and her parents owned the large Drapers' shop in the High Street where the Co-op Department Store now stands.

She became governor of St. Mary's Primary School, and also ran what was known, in those days, as "the mother's meeting", in the Parish Rooms of St. Mary's Church. The highlight of these meetings being the romantic novels which Hilda Marking read out loud to the other members.

Isaac on his part was a town councillor, a prominent Rotarian and Freemason, and a sidesman and Chairman of the Fabric Committee for St. Mary's Church.

They had two sons, Frank and Henry. Frank Marking, an aeronautical engineer, is now retired and living in Dorset.

Henry, who was knighted in 1978, lives at Strethall near Saffron Walden. He chose Law as his profession, and although his work has carried him to all four corners of the world, he has never really severed his ties with his home town.

Both boys went to Saffron Walden Grammar School. At the age of 16 Henry entered University College London. After a year studying for his intermediate exam he became an articled clerk in the offices of Cripps, Harries, Hall & Company in London.

Herbert Warner (right) 1958 on Market Day

205

At the age of 20 when war broke out in 1939, he entered the 2nd Battalion of the Sherwood Forresters and served in North Africa, Italy and the Middle East. In 1944 he was awarded the Military Cross.

After the War, and whilst he was still in the Middle East, he decided to learn Arabic and study Middle East history, politics and economics with a view to entering the Sudan Political Service.

However, after attending the various necessary interviews and being accepted for the Sudan Political Service, he chose instead to return home and carry on with his Law studies. A decision he has never regretted.

'Much to my surprise and everyone else's,' he says, 'I passed my exams in 1948.'

Henry Marking stayed on with Cripps, Harries, Hall & Company until 1949 when, "quite by chance" he got a job with British European Airways, later to become British Airways after amalgamation with B.O.A.C.

Sir Henry was Managing Director and Deputy Chairman of British Airways from 1972 until 1977 when he became Chairman of the British Tourist Authority until 1984.

Although, now at the age of 65, Sir Henry considers himself "semi-retired" he is still very actively engaged in the world of Big Business as Chairman of Rothman's U.K., and a member of the Board of both Rothman's International and Barclays International.

Despite his undoubted success in the business world, he is at heart very much a humanitarian. It was his deep concern for the sight of crippled children from the slums of Calcutta in India which brought him in contact with the Leonard Cheshire Foundation. A charity for which he has worked for almost 30 years.

He is now Vice Chairman of the Leonard Cheshire Foundation as well as being Chairman of the Holiday Care Service. This is an organisation offering advice to handicapped and disadvantaged people regarding cheap and convenient holiday accommodation.

Sitting in his warm and cheerful study at Strethall Hall, I asked Sir Henry if he enjoyed his life as a country gentleman, and he burst out laughing.

'I have never really thought of myself in that light!' he said. 'I don't shoot and I don't fish. True I have two horses, but I don't do much riding at the moment. But I like living in the country, and I like living here in Strethall, and I am devoted to Saffron Walden. I don't want to live anywhere else.'

Sir Henry and his brother Frank were born in the house next door to the butcher's shop on the corner of Museum Street, and Sir Henry recalls his early days with affection.

He says, 'I had a very happy childhood, because my mother and father were both wonderful people.'

'I remember the house quite well. What is now the tea shop was our dining room. And the carved over-mantel of the fireplace was made for my father about 1930, I think. I believe Mr. Ben Dix made it and did all that beautiful carving.

'Our sitting-room was next door to the butcher's shop, now it is all part of the china shop.

'My earliest memories are of the Muffin Man and water cart. The Muffin Man came round every Tuesday ringing his hand bell. He wore a green felt pad on his head on which he balanced his tray of muffins.

'The water cart came round in summer settling the dust in Church Street. Of course there was very little traffic in those days.'

Sir Henry showed me his grandfather's Profit and Loss Account for the year 1880, which he has now had framed.

It shows a gross profit of £104; wages £26; cost of keeping a horse £20, and rent of the meadow (probably Museum Meadow) £5. All in all, Isaac Marking made a net profit of £53 that year. Which doesn't sound very much these days but was obviously enough for the running of a highly successful business.

When asked what he thought about present-day Walden Sir Henry replied, 'I don't like some of the developments that are happening, and I think the Planners ought to pay more attention to the design of new buildings.'

About the prospect of Stansted becoming London's Third Airport, he said that, although he did not think people in Saffron Walden would be affected by the noise, personally he would be very sorry to see all the infrastructure which an airport inevitably brings in its wake.

207

He also feels that the Commissioner's report has not dealt adequately with the question of road access between Stansted and London.

'The route leading to the M11 from the parts of London where tourists stay,' he says, 'is along the Camden Road, Seven Sisters Road, Ferry Lane and Forest Road. These roads are already full to capacity and the whole of the traffic of North East London will grind to a halt if the inevitably increased airport traffic is added to the present congestion.

'It is no answer to say that passengers for Stansted would use a rail link. Many would not. And in any event the rail link would not be used for conveying cargo to and from Stansted.'

The demolition of Isaac Marking's old slaughterhouse marks the latest significant change in Museum Street.

For years it was a familiar, perhaps hardly loved, landmark, and now it is being replaced by a new development of houses.

The erection of these houses is another curious example of the Wheel of Fate turning full circle. At the beginning of the 19th century Thomas Bunting's house stood on what is now part of the churchyard.

Thomas Bunting was a glazier, and his house, as shown in Maynard's drawing, looks as if it was probably Tudor in origin, and quite large at that.

But in 1838, the churchwardens bought it from the land-lord, Lord Braybrooke, for £210, in order to demolish it and enlarge the churchyard cemetery. A case of the living having to make way for the dead.

So the new houses, if not exactly on the same site as Thomas Bunting's old house, will perhaps recompense for the misguided actions of those 19th century churchwardens.

——— · ———

Nos. 3 and 5 Museum Street are believed to have once been all one building, possibly much older than the 18th century brick facade we see today.

No.3, the office of the Conservative Association, is often referred to as "The Old Armoury". This is because from about 1888 until sometime during or just after the First World War, it was the headquarters of the Rifle Volunteers.

Previously the Armoury had been in Church Street, in one of the buildings belonging to the Sun Inn complex.

In 1920 the Conservative Association took over the premises. And a few years later, Lady Foot Mitchell, wife of Sir William Foot Mitchell, member of Parliament for Saffron Walden from 1924 until 1929, gave the Freehold to the Association.

Mr. Kenneth Baker has been Agent for the Saffron Walden Constituency Conservative Association since 1956.

Mr. Baker, who was born in Wales, says he has always been keenly interested in politics from a very early age. And he first became involved in the Conservative Cause on a purely voluntary basis soon after he came out of the army. Eventually this led to his decision to work for the Party in a professional capacity.

Since taking up his position as Agent he has worked for three members of parliament in the Saffron Walden Constituency; the late Lord Butler, the late Peter Kirk, and the present sitting member, Mr. Alan Hazelhurst. In addition his duties now include being Agent for M.E.P. David Curry.

Mr. Baker's right-hand man is – naturally enough – a woman. Mrs. Sheila Edgecombe became his secretary in September 1984, taking over from Miss Marjorie Jones, who worked for the Association both in a professional and voluntary capacity for over 38 years.

It would be impossible to talk about the Conservative Association without mentioning the late Lord Butler, whose memory is perpetuated in the name of the new Leisure Centre, and whose grave lies in the north-east corner of the churchyard.

R.A. Butler succeeded Sir William Foot Mitchell in 1929, and was M.P. for Saffron Walden until he received his life Peerage in 1965.

He was a man who loved the town and its people, and in return was deeply loved by them. And it is said he liked nothing better than to go down to the market on Tuesdays to chat with his farmer friends whenever he could.

'It is he' says Mr. Baker, 'who very largely shaped the thinking which has conditioned the political approach of the Saffron Walden Constituency Association.'

Next door to the Conservative Association office is, the Conservative Club.

It is difficult to trace the early history of the formation of the Conservative Club, but in September 1885, Colonel Alfred Crammer Byng of Quendon Hall; Major William Affleck King; George William Brewis and Martin Nockold, leased No.5 Museum Street from Georgina Mary Archer of Billericay for the purpose of providing premises for a Conservative Club (which had hitherto been meeting at The Rose and Crown – according to old Almanacks).

Georgina, a spinster, inherited the property from her mother, Mrs. Mary Jones, formerly Mrs. Archer, wife of George Archer.

No.5 had been in the Archer family since 1789, and strangely enough, appears to have been made over from a branch of the Jones family to the Archers.

On the 20th June 1894, the Club was enrolled as a member of the Association of Conservative Clubs. In 1923 the property was bought – probably with interest-free loans from members – from Georgina Archer for the sum of £1,050. A princely sum for those days, but a recent valuation estimates that the property is worth 200 times that sum now.

With a membership of 700 males and 400 affiliated lady members, it is, of course, very much a male-oriented concern. So much so that, on the only occasion Margaret Thatcher visited the Club – to lend support to Mr. Alan Hazelhurst – she entered the general bar with an apologetic 'I understand I'm not allowed in here!'

The general bar is a warm, smoke-filled, masculine domain with a one-armed bandit in the corner and the unmistakable noise of a game of snooker going on somewhere at the far end of the room.

Here, Roy Venables and his wife Frances, the Club Steward and Stewardess can be found.

Roy and Frances have been at the Conservative Club since July 1984. Previously Roy was a senior sales representative for Acrows.

Chairman of the Bar Committee is Mr. John Plumb, who farms at Wimbish and who has been a member of the Club for 30 years.

'It was my father who made me a member in the early 50s' says Mr. Plumb. 'But I didn't use the Club much in those days. The only time I came in here at all was to deliver the Almanack at Christmas time. But over the last 20 years I have become actively involved.

'My father was persuaded to join in 1950. He wasn't really a "club-man" but he always had an interest in Local Government.

'Eventually however, he became Chairman, and he and a few other members were mainly responsible for many of the alterations and improvements made to the premises in the early 70s'.

The alterations of which John Plumb speaks were occasioned by the departure of the N.F.U. who, for 14 years had leased the entire front of No.5 for their local branch headquarters.

With the general improvements the membership of the Club, which had hitherto remained quite modest, began to grow steadily.

A major improvement that John Plumb senior and his friends made was, extending the general bar to include the Billiards room. In the old days a game of snooker involved a draughty walk through an outside passage to the room where the billiard tables were kept. Not very pleasant on a cold winter's day.

Someone who remembers those days well is, Mr. Norman Hare of Wimbish, who joined the Club in 1928, and is now one of the Club's oldest members – and still playing snooker.

'When I first came here,' he says, 'they employed a Marker on Tuesdays to mark for the farmers. And there was a telephone with a handle that you turned to ring for a drink.'

Another long-established member is 81 year-old Mr. Eric Wright of Chelmsford.

Mr. Wright was born in South Road, Saffron Walden, and joined the Club at the age of 18 in 1923. A year later he won the Billiards' cup, and again in 1929.

Mr. Wright, who was a sales representative for Du Pont Brothers of Cambridge (later Eastern Area Manager) says that all his life he has been interested in politics and flying. (He got his 'A' licence for flying in 1930).

211

He also helped play a very active part in getting R.A. Butler in during the 1929 election.

'Captain Hunt was the Agent in those days, and he managed to get ahead of the Liberals by hiring all the village halls before they could get there.'

'I remember that night very well. The bar stayed open all night long. They didn't have a licence, but that didn't matter, and it's too late to do anything about it now.

'In the old days, of course, you really only had Liberals and Conservatives in the town, and nearly all the business men were members of the Conservative Club.

'The two billiard tables at the far end of the room are the original ones that have always stood there. And the old clock on the wall also. As far as I know that clock has never stopped, and always keeps excellent time. Even the two old wooden armchairs beneath it have been there ever since I can remember.'

Mr. Wright became Club Chairman in 1931, but left Saffron Walden in 1933. Nevertheless he still carried on being a member for a number of years after that. And even now continues to visit the Club once a month – weather permitting.

He is now Honorary Treasurer of Chelmsford Conservative Club and four years ago was awarded the Badge of Honour of the Association of Conservative Clubs for work both in the Club and for the Party. (A distinguished, all-England award, given to a very few).

Another member is Mr. Joe Darling, one-time Club Secretary, who has belonged to the Club for 15 years.

A retired airforce officer, Joe Darling was stationed near Saffron Walden in 1946 and married a girl from Widdington.

Since then he has been in and around the Saffron Walden area all the time, but is quite resigned to the fact that he will never be accepted as a local!

Squadron Leader Bruce Snook is another retired airforce officer also. He has been a member of the Club for 16 years, and for the past 13 has been Club Treasurer.

'I was stationed at Debden at one time,' he says, 'and we have lived in the area for quite a while. We realised long ago that Saffron Walden was an extremely pleasant place, and as we had made a lot of friends here, we decided that this was where we would live after I retired.'

When asked if he found the town had changed at all during the time he had known it, he said, 'Yes, and in my opinion not for the best. But I think one has to remember that probably I am taking a somewhat lop-sided point of view. We all like to think our own standards should apply. And you must either expand or die, and I don't want to see Saffron Walden die. It is a lovely little town with lots of interest and lots of fun.'

A comparative newcomer to Saffron Walden is the Club Secretary, Mr. Frank Harrison. Mr Harrison, a retired Civil Servant, was born in Cambridge, but now lives in Saffron Walden, and has been a member of the Conservative Club for seven years.

No.5 still retains many elegant 18th century features, and the graceful staircase and entrance hall are not without a certain stylishness.

The Lounge Bar (ladies permitted) is a large, comfortable, welcoming room with splendid high ceilings and more than a hint of gracious living.

Nos.7 and 9 Museum Street are two early 18th century timber-framed and plastered cottages.

Outside No.7 you will find a wooden bench with an invitation to sit down should you feel so inclined. A very welcome gesture to the footsore and weary, and especially pleasant on a warm, sunny day.

It was Mrs. Anne Richings' idea to put the seat there in the first place. She and her daughter, 9 year-old Cherry, live at No.7, and apart from a tiny enclosed yard at the back of the cottage, there is virtually no garden to the house.

As the front of the cottage gets all the sun when it shines (or did before the houses opposite were built) she thought it would be nice if other people could enjoy the sunshine as well as Cherry and herself.

The bench, like the chimney pots – which are now used as flower pots – has its own history.

Mrs. Richings, who has lived in Saffron Walden for 18 years, bought the bench when Junior House School in Audley Road closed down.

'We practically furnished the whole of the house we were living in at the time for about £50 from the stuff we bought at the Junior House School Auction Sale. The bench was one long school bench which we sawed in half to make two.

'The chimney pots I bought for 10/- (50p) each from the Auction Sale at the Rose & Crown after it was burned down. They are now scattered all over Walden. We have lived in various houses in the town, and wherever we have been, I have used them as flower pots and left them behind when we moved.'

Tiny cottage No.7 might be, but in one corner of its backyard there actually stands a Victorian Folly – half a flint tower with a pointed Gothic doorway. A strange, picturesque little building whose history remains unexplained.

Some people still call No.7 "Cobbler's Cottage", because it was here that "Snobby" Wright, the cobbler lived from 1839 until about 1930. ("Snobby" being the old name for a shoe-mender).

Albert Wright was born in Henham in 1863, fourth in a generation of boot and shoemakers. He came to Saffron Walden in 1887, and according to the rating lists spent most of his working life at No.7 Museum Street.

His workshop was one of the two front rooms of the cottage, and the lean-to outbuilding, now Anne's kitchen, was probably where he stored all his materials.

Snobby was a well-known character as well as being a boot and shoemaker. He was Sunday School Superintendent and Deacon of Abbey Lane Congregational Church, and Secretary of the Shepherd's Friendly Society.

Before Snobby came to live at No.7, the cottage had, for many years, been a boarding house run by Mrs. Georgina Cowell, and perhaps this explains the extraordinary rabbit warren of extremely tiny little rooms in the cottage.

Immediately adjacent to No.9 is a brick wall, which at one time enclosed the playground of Museum Street Infants School.

The original Nos.11 and 13 Museum Street were two timber-framed and jettied cottages. Wonderful examples of what appears to have been medieval architecture, demolished in 1894 to make way for the school playground.

Afred Ernest "Snobby" Wright in his workshop

Museum Street School was erected in 1817, built from the proceeds of subscriptions of between 2/- (10p) and £100. And if records are accurate it would appear to be the forerunner of Castle Street School and not exclusively for infants.

Later, in 1837, Rating Lists describe it as "Girls' National School". This description continues until 1848. In the meantime, Castle Street School (now St. Mary's was built in 1843 for boys only in the first instance.

In the records of 1849 the Museum Street School appears as "Infants" and continues as such right up to the 1960s when it was purchased by the Museum to be used as a Lecture Room.

Now we come to Castle Hill Tennis Club. "New Members Welcome" says a notice outside the Pavilion. In the old days however, this was not always so.

In the early decades of this century, Castle Hill Tennis Club was, to put it mildly, rather exclusive. One lady, who in her youth had been a keen tennis player, put it rather more bluntly when I asked if she had ever been a member.

'Good gracious no! We were Trade, and they were much too posh to have anything to do with Trade!'

So it would seem that, in those halcyon days when everyone knew their place, Castle Hill Tennis Club was run exclusively for the wealthy and professional people of the town!

Little Marjorie Cornell (Mrs. Frank Sutton) who lived for a while in Museum Yard, loved to stand and watch the ladies and gentlemen playing tennis.

'In those days the courts were grass. And in the summer when they had matches, they would have trestle tables covered with snowy white cloths, laid out with the most beautiful food. Oh I can see it now! It all looked so marvellous.

'Sometimes, when the ball was hit out, I would go and fetch it for them. Once, I was actually asked to hold a player's racquet. I was absolutely thrilled. That was my first introduction to tennis!'

(Later, Marjorie Cornell became quite an accomplished tennis player herself.)

'... but under the turf of the Lawn Tennis Club and Museum grounds, there awaits the archaeologist a marvellous opportunity to uncover a complex of buildings associated with medieval manor house – centre of the de Bohun's estates in Walden.'

So writes Mrs. Dorothy Cromarty in an article on "Chepying Walden" (the early name for Saffron Walden) 1381–1420, for the Essex Journal in 1967.

Mrs. Cromarty has researched into the early history of Saffron Walden with painstaking thoroughness, and few would disagree with her findings, but it would be a brave and headstrong archaeologist who would have the temerity to start digging-up Bury Hill!

The secrets which lie beneath the turf of the inner and out Bailey of the old Castle had better remain undisclosed. Because it is here, in 1831, that the third Lord Braybrooke erected the large Tudor-style brick building which houses Saffron Walden Museum.

But it is interesting to note that the present entrance to the Museum grounds appears to correspond to the west gate of the old manor of the de Bohun's.

Referring to Mrs. Cromarty again – 'an un-used lane (Museum Street) led from Castlestret (Castle Street) towards the west gate of the manor, and from it one could enter the cemetry on the other side through a stone stile.'

The Museum

The position of the stile according to Mrs. Cromarty's map, is the same as the position of the steps at the north-east corner of the churchyard, still very much in use!

It was the founders of the Natural History Society who prevailed upon Lord Braybrooke to build the Museum House as a general amenity to the town. And in the beginning it housed other cultural societies as well as the Natural History Society.

In reality, the Natural History Society at that time was another exclusive Club, and it was not until the 12th May 1835 that its Collection was opened as a Museum. Even then, admittance was very tightly controlled.

During the 1860s however, it was decided to open it to the general public. And eventually in 1879, the whole building was taken over by the Museum.

Because the founders and other local people were connected with various missionary activities throughout the world, the Museum had a strong ethnographical bias from the outset.

A prominent member of the Natural History Society at that time was Hannibal Dunn, who had a brother living in South Africa. The brother, on hearing of the proposed Museum promptly went out and shot everything in sight. The result was an inundation of hundreds of tropical animals for the Museum Trustees to cope with.

Some of the animals were distributed to other museums, but the Natural History Society kept most, and these formed the major part of the Collection in the early days.

Pride of the exhibition was the elephant. Alas, poor Jumbo is no longer with us.

His was an ignominious end, considering that, despite his African origins, he was the centre of attraction in the Indian Pavilion at the Great Exhibition 1851. For, at that time he was unique – the only elephant in a museum in the whole of the country.

It was in 1958, during a complete reorganisation of the Museum that it was decided to "dispose" of Jumbo. He had been on display for 125 years, 'under conditions not exactly ideal,' says the Museum Curator, Mr. Len Pole, 'and I imagine his skin was beginning to show signs of wear.'

Controversy raged in the local Press. Jumbo was much loved by everyone who had visited the Museum as a child. But it was no use. In 1960 Jumbo was sent with some other large mammals, including a rhinocerous, to people, known to the Museum Trustees, who lived in Bath.

Jumbo was put on display in their back garden, to slowly and silently rot away, and sink gently into oblivion.

He was mourned by many. Especially by those exiles who, on revisiting their home town, made a pilgrimage to the Museum just to see him once again!

The Museum Collection covers a wide range of subjects, and is growing steadily all the time. So much so that plans are now underway to build a second level in the Great Hall.

Mr. Len Pole has been Curator of the Museum for over ten years, and in 1982 was elected a Fellow of the Museums Association, an honour awarded to members of the Association for services given beyond the workaday duties of a curator.

A Londoner by birth, he is a graduate of Bristol University and holds a degree in psychology and a post-graduate diploma in social anthropology.

For three years he was Assistant Curator to the Museum of Accra in Ghana before coming to Saffron Walden.

Assistant Curator Sheila Jordain has also worked at the Museum for approximately ten years.

Sheila, who was born in Plymouth, now lives in Cambridge, and has a degree in history and an A.M.A. diploma in Art History, has also worked at the Bow Museum in Barnard Castle, County Durham.

The high quality of the Museum Collection brought Sheila to Saffron Walden. Especially as it includes the things that interest her most – the Applied Arts, particularly Ceramics and Glass.

Although she is responsible for the whole of the Applied Arts Section, Sheila says her first love is really Ceramics, particularly English Delftware and English Creamware.

When asked if she ever feels nervous at handling so many valuable objects , she laughs. 'No, you get used to it. We are always very careful of course, and when we carry them around we always pack them in boxes.

'We take every precaution we can, and if you do that and you do have the misfortune to have an accident, then at least you know it is not through carelessness.

'Even so, I must admit, I do *not* like shifting the glass posset pot!' (A unique piece of 17th century glass).

Sheila also helps with other parts of the Museum Collection, and was recently in charge of the reorganisation of the Costume Gallery.

'Here I was very fortunate,' she says, 'because I had a lot of volunteers with art school training to help me.'

Whilst talking to Sheila, sitting in her workroom – a large expanse of behind-the-scenes historical clutter – my eyes were drawn to a wall clock of abundant proportions, exquisitely inlaid with mother-of-pearl.

Sheila pointed to the inscription on the clock – it read – "Presented to Robert Ship on 20th October 1840, by the Saffron Walden Agricultural Society for bringing up his family and claiming the least Parochial Relief."

Poor, proud Robert Ship! What a reflection of the times!

Another member of the Museum staff is Lousie Bacon.

Louise, another Londoner by birth, has diplomas in Archaeology and Archaeological Conservation, and is the Museum's Conservator.

Her job is to preserve the Museum's Collection for posterity. This involves cleaning, repairing and stabilizing the objects from further deterioration.

She says it is also important to see that the environment of the object on display is also right. This means correct temperature, humidity and the actual display materials themselves. For example there are some woods which cannot be used for background material because they give off organic acid vapours.

Louise has been a Conservator for 15 years, working in various Museums at home and in exotic places like Mexico, Peru and Thailand.

She came to Saffron Walden Museum five years ago, 'because it has a fine, varied collection and an extremely good reputation.!'

Apart from the odd student who helps out occasionally, Louise works completely alone.

When I interviewed her she was repairing one half of a huge clam shell which normally stands outside the Museum door. A few years ago it had been smashed by vandals, despite its heavy weight (over half a hundredweight) and just recently it had been damaged yet again. This time an unfortunate motorist had reversed into it.

I asked Louise the same question I had asked Sheila – if she ever felt nervous handling such precious things?

'Obviously I am dealing with historically important objects. If I make a mistake they are ruined for all time. That is one of the responsibilities which goes with job. But if you can't accept responsibility – don't be a Conservator!'

'Strangely enough, it is mostly women who do this job! Having said that though – I must add – my behaviour is completely different at home. I drop things and break them, and I *never* repair anything!'

Although the Museum boasts only three fulltime staff, there are many willing, unpaid volunteers who work quietly in the background, and two part-time members of staff.

Mrs. Maureen Evans works in a non-curatorial capacity as press officer, and Don Hefferon – a professional sculptor – helps in a pratical capacity. Recently, he has just completed the base for Wallace the Lion, star of the forthcoming sesquicentennial celebrations.

——— · ———

Close by the entrance to the grounds of the Museum is, Museum yard, one of those delightful, almost forgotten backwaters which add so much to the charm of Saffron Walden.

Here a cluster of tiny, late 18th century timber-framed and plaster cottages enjoy friendly privacy. Each cottage has its own miniscule garden, just big enough to sit in on a warm, sunny day.

Mrs. Sybil Hagger has lived at No.1 Museum Yard for four years now, and although she was born at Wendens Ambo, she does not consider herself "a local".

An ex-pupil of Cambridge House School, she remembers the formidable Miss Gowletts very well.

Museeum Yard

She comes from a very old local farming family, and is the daughter of Henry Duke who farmed at Wendens Hall in the early decades of this century.

Like so many farmer's daughters, she married a farmer, Christopher Hagger, who was born at Gt. Bowsers Farm, Ashdon, and whose family later farmed Bulse Farm, Wendens Ambo.

After Christopher Hagger retired, he and Sybil went to live at Theydon Bois, but when he died a few years ago, Sybil came to live in Museum Yard, next door to her sister.

Across the way from Museum Yard are Nos.2, 4 and 6 Museum Street, a terrace of tall, narrow, three storey grey gault brick cottages.

Although there are no notes as to the actual date of these cottages, their appearance suggests early 19th century weavers' cottages.

No.2 is the home of 75 year-old Mr. Alfred Clark and his wife Doris. They have lived at this address for over 40 years and have seen many changes in the street during that time.

They miss the old days. 'People are not like they used to be,' says Doris, who was born at No.70 Castle Street 70 years ago.

'Once I knew everybody in Castle Street, but now most of the old people have gone. There used to be so much going on, now it's rather quiet and altogether different.'

Alfred was born at Debden, and until he was called up during the second World War, worked at Abbotts Farm, Debden, (later the farm became part of the aerodrome).

He and Doris met in the queue at the Walden Cinema one Saturday night. They married in 1940, and Doris, who worked at Gold Street Laundry, lived with her mother in Castle Street until Alfred came out of the army.

After he was demobbed, Alfred went to work for Myhills in Gold Street where he stayed until he retired.

Next door, No.4, will be remembered by some as the establishment of Edward Henry Kenny, "Proprietor of Cattle Medicines". Edward Kenny lived at No.4 from 1897 until 1920.

Whilst No.6, was another of Mrs. Marjorie Sutton's childhood homes after her parents, Charlie and Nell Cornell, moved from No.75 Castle Street.

Mrs. Sutton says, 'I used to love the little house in Museum Street. I remember the copper was in the living room and on washing days the whole room was full of steam.

'Of course the lavatory was outside – they always were in those days – but at least in Museum Street we did have one to ourselves. And mother, who always liked to make things look pretty, planted nasturtions around it.'

Nos. 11 and 15 Museum Street are survivors. The only examples of early 15th century architecture left standing in the Street.

Originally they were all one building, built quite possibly, when the number of dyeworks situated in this part of the Castle bailey was increasing rapidly because of the expansion of the Saffron Industry in the town at that time.

We must remember that in the 15th century Bury Hill was a complex of timber-framed cottages and building belonging to the manor farm.

Referring to Mrs. Dorothy Cromarty – Essex Journal of 1967 – these buildings would have been interspersed with gardens and pastures, and other open spaces which – during the late 14th and early 15th century – became rapidly filled up by the vats and sheds of the dyers.

Water for the process of dyeing would probably have been obtained from the deep well in the precincts of the Keep. So all in all, the whole area inside the Castle bailey would have been highly industrialised.

In which case, it is reasonable to assume that the wealthy dyers built themselves handsome houses just outside the Castle bailey, and that Nos.11 to 15 did at one time belong to a prosperous dyer.

Although we are not concerned with the Church at this stage in our walk around Walden, we must make a point of calling in at the Rectory before it ceases to be the Rectory.

At the moment, the Rectory is the subject of raging controversy, and Canon Harlow and his wife will shortly be moving to another part of the town.

Cannon Harlow says 'I'm all for building houses in the garden of the Rectory'. (The subject of all the controversy). And – warming to the subject – 'and yes – I think there should be another car park, and personally I wouldn't mind it being on the Common!'

The 1851 Census tells us that the Rev. Ralph Clutton and his wife Isabella, lived at the Rectory with their four children and four servants (nurse, cook, housemaid and nurserymaid).

The last house in Museum Street is No.17. Tall, and spare of embellishment, it brings an atmosphere of Edwardian respectability to its near neighbours.

Built for the curate of St. Mary's, and known for many years as "the curate's house", it is now an Accountant's office.

Mrs. Betty Hart at No.61 Castle Street, remembers this house as the home of Mr. Williams the Jobmaster who kept the Livery Stables down Freshwell Street.

She describes him as "a short plump man, with a little pointed beard, looking a bit like King Edward VII."